Money Lessons

Money Lessons

*How to Manage Your Finances to
Get the Life You Want*

LISA CONWAY-HUGHES

PENGUIN LIFE

AN IMPRINT OF

PENGUIN BOOKS

PENGUIN LIFE

UK | USA | Canada | Ireland | Australia
India | New Zealand | South Africa

Penguin Life is part of the Penguin Random House group of companies
whose addresses can be found at global.penguinrandomhouse.com.

First published 2019
001

Set in 13.5/16 pt Garamond MT Std
Typeset by Jouve (UK), Milton Keynes
Printed and bound in Great Britain by Clays Ltd, Elcograf S.p.A.

A CIP catalogue record for this book is available from the British Library

ISBN: 978–0–241–37934–9

www.greenpenguin.co.uk

MIX
Paper from
responsible sources
FSC
www.fsc.org
FSC® C018179

Penguin Random House is committed to a
sustainable future for our business, our readers
and our planet. This book is made from Forest
Stewardship Council® certified paper.

I dedicate this book to my children – Jago & Kiki xx

CONTENTS

INTRODUCTION

What's the Point of Being Financially Savvy?

We can always find excuses not to make positive financial choices. Life tempts us with one-click shopping, a taxi is only a few taps away and our lives are so hectic that popping out to buy lunch over taking a packed lunch has become the norm. In addition, life seems to continually give us signals that money is a taboo subject. British society teaches us that it is bad to talk about money at home, in the workplace and even with our closest friends. It's also acceptable (even funny) to admit that you are bad at maths. Maths and money are so often filed in the same mental compartment that it then somehow also feels okay to be bad with money. Added to all this is the fact that the financial industry is notorious for using mind-boggling jargon and making things complicated, so that when it comes to our money we often find ourselves making choices that actually leave us worse off than before.

The purpose behind this book is to help you take your first steps towards being financially in control. The short-term consequences of good money habits are rewarding and hopefully liberating. However, the long-term impact of financial savviness is life-changing. It's the difference between living a life where you use money to achieve the things that are important to you – that make you happy – rather than money dictating the type of life that you lead.

If you look up 'savvy' in the dictionary it is described as:

'Shrewd and knowledgeable; having common sense and good judgement'

When it comes to money, no matter your age, the majority of people wouldn't count themselves as being 'financially savvy'. In fact, most people make financial decisions on a day-to-day basis as questions about spending present themselves, and stick their head in the sand when it comes to thinking about longer-term finances. However, if you stop for just a moment and ask your brain to think about money, what are the questions that pop into your mind? Perhaps they go something like this:

– 'Will I ever be out of debt?'

– 'How am I ever going to buy a house?'

- 'Will I ever be able to retire?'

- 'Am I stuck in this job for ever?'

If these questions leave you feeling stressed, or with a feeling of dread in your stomach, you aren't alone. For many people, money worries are the last thing that they think about at night. So how do we get from being financially scared to financially savvy?

For me, the definition of being financially savvy is having freedom from money worries. Not just living hand to mouth, being in debt and having very little in the way of savings. It's the freedom that comes with having the knowledge and confidence to make sound financial decisions that can help you to build (over time) your dream life. It's feeling comfortable talking, thinking and doing when it comes to money, having confidence in your own abilities to manage your finances. This is good financial wellbeing.

When I have the discussion with my clients about their financial wellbeing, very often they haven't given it a thought.

The reason why is because it is not something that we are used to doing. School and sometimes family background teaches us to get our head down and work hard regardless of whether we're heading towards the destination we actually want. How many people take the first graduate job going on a meagre salary, only to realize ten years later that they are in an industry that doesn't interest them and their income hasn't grown the way they thought? How many have followed the financial choices and career paths that would please their parents but not them? How many don't know their own worth when it comes to the money they should be earning? If you don't know your own worth and the value of your time (after all, we only have a finite amount of it), how will you build the life that you deserve? If you are wasting the money you earn on unnecessary things or even indulging in the excesses of modern life, will you ever keep up with yourself? Not just financially (debt is very draining) but also in your career: will you become trapped in a job you hate because of the salary?

The need to assign time to focus on self-care and personal development has become a given. How does the time you spend on taking care of yourself compare with the time you spend on your financial wellbeing? When so much of our mental wellbeing is tied up with our money, should we all be doing more? If you spent an hour a month nurturing your finances for the next twelve months, how would you feel this time next year? What would be different?

This book is your opportunity to take a step back and spend some time mapping out the future you want, identifying what will make you happy and how your finances can enable you to do this. This point is really important as most people look at it the other way round. Their finances dictate their life and their happiness – which to me just doesn't make sense. Money should be the tool that you use to achieve your dreams – not the thing that holds you back from reaching them.

As time goes by, your aims in life and the things that are important to you will change, and so too will your financial plan, so it's important to make sure you enjoy the process along the way!

Setting Financial Goals

Setting long-term goals when it comes to money is scary in itself, especially if you haven't done anything like it before. The key to good goal-setting is to chunk it into realistic and obtainable mini goals if you are initially struggling to 'think big'. This will help the goal to instantly feel more achievable and will help you to meet this goal in the short term. Remember: just because a goal has been set, it doesn't mean that it is set in stone. Goals need to be flexible so that as your life changes and your priorities change over time, you can also adapt your goals.

For example, when I was in my late twenties I presumed that by my mid-thirties I would be feeling grown-up and that moving out of London would be important to me. Now that I am in my late thirties, I realize that staying in London is actually very important to me and so I have had to change my goals about the type of home I wanted to buy accordingly.

The first thing when it comes to setting goals is *not*

to listen to those niggling doubts in the back of your mind: 'That's never going to happen', 'I don't know anyone my age who's done that before' or 'Why bother, I won't stick to it.'

Goals are there to stretch you, to motivate you and, most importantly, to change your life. Therefore you need to be brave and even step out of your comfort zone in order to consider what you actually want out of life.

On p. 8 you will find a table that I fill out with all of my clients when we first start working together. It will help you to focus on what you want at each stage of your life. You then review this annually and track your progress along the way – ticking off those milestones as you achieve them. Believe me, it will be so rewarding to look back in ten years' time and reflect on how you have smashed your goals!

To help with identifying your goals, write down the following:

Five things that make you happy

1) ....

2) ....

3) ....

4) ....

5) ....

How many of these are you doing already?

1) ....

2) ....

3) ....

4) ....

5) ....

Now fill in the goals table while holding these answers in mind.

Before you file this goal-setting task as 'mentally done', take time to reflect. Perhaps sleep on it to ensure that it is really what you want to achieve. It is so important to get this right as this exercise will help you to shape the direction of your financial plan. Are any of the goals in there because they are what you feel you 'should do' or because they would impress certain people? Do these goals help you to work towards your definition of happy?

I love meeting people who have really gone against the grain and carved out the life that they want, irrespective of what society says. For example, I have a friend who loves the sun and took the plunge to change her life and her business. Rather than waiting to retire to the sun, she bought a place in Portugal. She changed her coaching business to be remote, and clients even started flying out to see her. She downsized her house to a flat

	Career	Property	Family and Personal
Twenties			
Thirties			
Forties			
Fifties			
Sixties			
Seventies			
Beyond			

really close to Heathrow and every month now spends two weeks in London and two weeks abroad. She has made the life she wanted for herself.

A colleague of mine loves travel. He started off by booking up budget airline tickets to Europe as soon as they were released. He then spent most weekends travelling around Europe on his motorbike. Each weekend he would start off where he finished the weekend before. After a few years, he had worked his way across the whole of Europe and started to want to travel further afield. This led to him planning two sabbaticals of three months each. In the first one he motorcycled from the top of South America all the way down to the southern tip of Argentina and took the trip of a lifetime to Antarctica. The second one covered the Middle East and India. My life isn't that flexible these days, but I find these examples so inspiring and they help me to remember to think outside of the box when I am considering my own goals.

On p. 10 is an example of a table filled out with things that I hear most often.

Did you put any of these goals in your own table? Or were you surprised how your answers differed?

We will come back to your own goals table as we work our way through this guide together.

Money Vision Board

Making a money vision board is a very personal thing and what goes on it depends on what motivates you.

	Career	Property	Family and Personal
Twenties	Stay in role until earning £25K	Renting	Three-month sabbatical
Thirties	Start looking for a management role and expect earnings to be £40–£45K	Buy first property	Get married mid-thirties – kids? Shared maternity/paternity leave
Forties	Set up own business – aim for earnings £75–£80K	Buy family home	Have one winter and one summer holiday
Fifties			Help kids through university
Sixties	Retire mid-sixties and sell business	Buy a home abroad	Help kids out with property purchase
Seventies			Travel lots
Beyond		Downsize/sell a property	

Personally, I love doing them, so I make it a task for each December to spend time creating a very beautiful board. I gather *loads* of magazines and over a glass of wine (or two . . .) look for pictures/words that summarize how I would like my life to pan out and what I need to do over the next twelve months to achieve or work towards these goals. Some targets are very practical, about where I live, how much money I have. Others are more indulgent – usually the holidays I would like to go on that year or a fancy meal out at a good restaurant.

What I love about doing vision boards is it gives you the freedom to think big. It doesn't matter if your conscious mind thinks it is likely to happen or not. I love looking back on them to reflect how my goals have changed, but also to see which ones I have actually achieved, which always gives me a boost of motivation to keep going. Grab yourself a big piece of paper or card, a stack of magazines, and just cut out and stick down those images and words that really jump out at you to create a snapshot of your financial goals for the next twelve months.

Money Mindfulness

Understanding what has shaped your money attitudes can help you to get to the bottom of all those bad habits. Do you naturally switch off when the subject of money appears? Do you try to control people with money? Are you scared to spend? Perhaps you can't stop spending?

Maybe even the idea of opening a letter from the bank makes you want to hibernate?

How would you react to the following situations?

- A letter from the bank arrives with URGENT stamped in red on the front.

- Your partner asks you to sit down and discuss money.

- Your friend asks you how much you earn.

- You get an unexpected inheritance of £50,000.

Now think about how your life experiences so far have shaped these natural reactions. Consider these questions:

1) What money false truths do you tell yourself? Why?

2) How has your upbringing shaped your money beliefs? Did your parents argue about money? Was money taboo?

3) What have you picked up along the way from other important people in your life?

4) Have you had any really bad or really good money experiences?

Now that you have thought about it, are there any unhealthy money beliefs and habits that you would like to change? What little things can you do to start to improve your own internal money dialogue? It doesn't matter if the changes are small. Tiny baby steps all add up. What is most important is that the changes are easy to stick to. There's no point in a financial crash diet!

Can you take a moment to reframe any of the answers you gave above in a more positive light? Perhaps instead of beating yourself up about a bad decision a few years back to take a job with a lower salary, which has left you racking up the debt on credit cards, you can think: *Well, I do really love my job, I was brave and took a chance, but now perhaps I can make a goal to address getting a pay rise or start looking for a similar job with a competitor for a better salary.*

When we start to change the way we think and feel about money, and the stories we tell ourselves about our money, we can start to change our financial behaviours for the better.

Getting Your Head Round Tax

Before we get going, it's important to do a quick crash course in tax in order for you to know the most accurate figures when doing your calculations throughout the following chapters. Tax is a compulsory contribution we all must pay to the state; it helps to pay for things like the fire service, our healthcare, etc. You pay tax on your income, when you buy commodities (VAT), when you buy a property (stamp duty), when you sell an investment at a profit and even when you die. Most clients that I meet do not really have a great grasp of tax, so here is my whistle-stop tour of how tax works!

How Does Income Tax Work?

'In this world nothing can be said to be certain, except death and taxes'
Benjamin Franklin

The first tax bracket is 0%. This is called the personal allowance and most people can benefit from earning £11,850 (tax year 2018/19) before you start to pay tax. From this point, you start to pay basic rate tax, which is currently 20%. You pay 20% all the way up to earnings of £46,350 (2018/19). This is then the start of the higher rate tax, which is

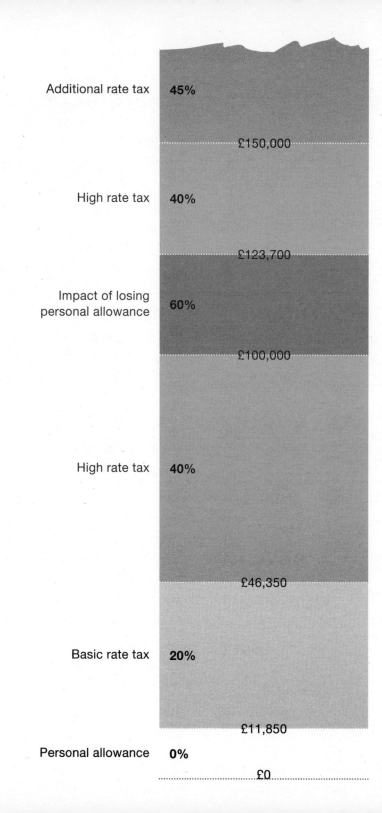

Additional rate tax **45%**

£150,000

High rate tax **40%**

£123,700

Impact of losing
personal allowance **60%**

£100,000

High rate tax **40%**

£46,350

Basic rate tax **20%**

£11,850

Personal allowance **0%**

£0

40%. The 40% tax threshold ends at earnings of £150,000. From this point you become an additional rate tax payer, which is 45%.

There is one extra thing you need to know if you earn over £100,000. For every £1 you earn over £100,000 you lose 50p of your personal allowance and so you start to pay tax earlier.

All of the tax brackets and rates mentioned above are based on the figures for 2018/19. If you would like to check what current rates are, you can do this online at www.gov.uk/income-tax-rates. Listen out too for the chancellor's Autumn Budget every October and the Spring Statement in March.

Other Taxes to Know About
Dividends tax

Dividend payments can be paid to you if you own shares in a company. It is common for company owners to take dividends out of their company on top of their earnings, on which they pay income tax.

You are allowed to earn £2,000 in dividends before you pay tax. Above this, the rate of tax that you pay depends on your income tax bracket. Don't forget that if your dividends take you into the next tax bracket you will pay some tax in each.

Tax Bracket	Tax Rate On Dividends
Basic Rate	7.5%
Higher Rate	32.5%
Additional Rate	38.1%

Capital gains tax

This is tax that you pay when assets that you own go up in value. Tax is paid when you sell the asset. It is paid on the gain you made rather than the money you receive.

You don't pay tax when you sell your main residence or if you transfer assets between spouses or civil partners. ISAs, UK Government Gilts, Premium Bonds and winnings (from betting or lottery) don't usually incur capital gains tax either.

Like with income tax, capital gains tax also has a tax-free allowance. The capital gains tax-free allowance is £11,700 (2018/19). So if you make gains below this amount then you do not pay tax.

If you are a higher rate income tax payer, you pay capital gains tax at the following rates:

— 28% on residential property, i.e. a buy-to-let investment

— 20% on other assets

If you are a basic rate tax payer you pay capital gains tax at the following rates:

— 18% on residential property, i.e. a buy-to-let investment

— 10% on other assets

Please be aware though that if you make a large enough gain, you could end up paying some tax at the basic rate and then the rest at the higher rate.

Inheritance tax

Inheritance tax is paid on the value of your assets when you die. You don't pay inheritance tax if the total value of your estate is less than £325,000 or if you leave everything to a spouse/civil partner, a charity or a community amateur sports club.

If you leave your home to your children or grandchildren, the £325,000 threshold is increased to £450,000.

If your assets are above the threshold then you pay tax at 40%. (We will cover inheritance tax in more detail in chapter 8.)

1

GET BUDGETING!

Setting Your Ideal Budget

The secret to budgeting is that it needs to be honest. Not what you think it should be or wish it could be, but what it really is. A good budget is the foundation of all your financial wellbeing and will be the difference between staying on track with your goals or not. In this chapter I am going to show you how to plan a budget and stick to it.

Let's start with the steps below so you can plan and record your own budget on pp. 24–7.

You need to first gather at least six months' but ideally twelve months' worth of bank statements and record all your expenditure in a spreadsheet. If you don't get physical statements, all the better – I prefer to download them as Excel files directly from my online banking to save time! Once you have everything together, do the following:

1) Merge them all into one Excel file.

2) Sort them by amount (click on the data tab, then sort, with the highest first).

3) One by one, add all the essential outgoings that happen each month (mortgage/rent/gas/ electricity/water/phone/gym membership/ Netflix, etc.) to your budget planner on p. 24, then delete them from your spreadsheet. The remaining things you have spent money on then need to be categorized into the groups that you will find on the budget planner, for example:

   • Food Shopping
   • Holidays
   • Socializing
   • Books/Magazines
   • Clothes
   • Hair
   • Beauty etc.

4) For each category you have, divide it by twelve and add it to the *monthly* column of your budget planner. Note that this is just analysing where your money goes rather than how to spend it going forward.

5) If you look down the columns of the budget planner, are there any that are blank which you

think you are going to need to start spending on in the next twelve months? If so, add your best guess for this amount into the appropriate column.

6) When you are adding in your income, don't forget to make sure that you are adding in your income after tax – this is known as your net income. The most accurate place to get this from is your payslip. This will ensure you have taken into account all deductions, i.e. pension, student loan, childcare vouchers, etc. If you are self-employed and unsure of your net income, you might be best to speak to your accountant. (See p. 14 for a handy guide to tax.)

7) Analyse – is there anything that shocks you? Where are you spending too much? Which areas would be easy to cut back on? What has this exercise taught you? Write your thoughts in the ANALYSE box after the budget planner.

MONTHLY INCOME	Client 1	Client 2
Net Income From Employment / Self-employment		
Income From Savings & Investments		
Other Income		
Benefits (Child Benefit, Child Tax Credits & Income Support)		
TOTAL		

OUTGOINGS	Monthly	Annual

Regular Household Bills

	Monthly	Annual
Mortgage/Rent		
Buildings & Contents Insurance		
Bank Account Fee		
Overdraft Cost		
Council Tax		
Water Rates/Meter		
Gas		
Electricity		
Oil		
Household Maintenance		
Garden Maintenance		
Cleaning Products/Cleaner		
Home Phone		
Internet		
TV Licence		
Mobile Phone		

OUTGOINGS (cont.) | Monthly | Annual

Insurance

	Monthly	Annual
Level Term		
Mortgage Payment Protection		
Mortgage Term		
Pet		
Travel		
Private Medical Insurance		
Dental Insurance		
Healthcare Cashplans		
Gas & Plumbing/Boiler Cover		

Food

	Monthly	Annual
Food and Household Shopping		
Meals at Work		

Travel

	Monthly	Annual
Breakdown Cover/Roadside Recovery		
Rail/Bus/Coach/Taxi		
Car Maintenance		
Car Insurance		
Car Tax		
Parking		
Petrol/Diesel		

Debt

	Monthly	Annual
Car Loan Repayments		
Personal Loan Repayments		
Family Loan Repayments		
Credit Card Repayments		

OUTGOINGS (cont.) Monthly Annual

Savings

	Monthly	Annual
Financial Adviser Retainer		
Lump Sum Savings		
Mini Cash ISAs		
Investments		
Buying Shares		
Pension Payments		

Family Costs

	Monthly	Annual
Childcare/Play Schemes		
Babysitting		
Children's Travel		
Laundry/Dry Cleaning		
Nappies/Baby Extras		
Pocket Money		
School Fees		
School Meals		
School Trips		
Pet Food		
Pet Costs		
Satellite/Digital TV Subscription		
Fitness/Sports/Gym		
Dentistry		
Haircuts		
Optical Bills		

OUTGOINGS (cont.)   Monthly   Annual

One Offs

	Monthly	Annual
Christmas		
Summer Holiday		
Winter Holiday		
Accountant		
Sofa/Kitchen/TV		
Wedding Expenses		

Other

	Monthly	Annual
Regular Charity Donations		
Fun/Social/Eating out		
Newspapers & Magazines		
Clothes		
Beauty		

	Monthly	Annual
TOTAL OUTGOINGS		

	Monthly	Annual
TOTAL DISPOSABLE INCOME		

Analyse

....

....

....

....

....

....

....

....

....

....

....

If your budget was positive
(you spend less than you earn)

Well done for spending less than you earn. This is exactly where I want you to be! However, perhaps there is still room for improvement? Could you free up even more money to work towards those goals you set at the beginning of this book?

If you are zero
(you spend exactly what you earn)

Not bad, but definitely room for improvement. It is important that you spend more time on the budget planner working out what savings and cutbacks you can make. Compromises will have to be made but remind yourself of the goals you have set, what you are working towards and why you are doing this.

If you are negative
(you spend more than you earn)

This is not the financial position you want to be in, but don't beat yourself up – the most important thing is that you've worked out the damage. It is really important that you spend a lot of time working out what sacrifices and cutbacks can be made to ensure you aren't spending more than you earn.

Extreme Example Case Study: FIRE

This stands for Financial Independence Retire Early – or working because you want to rather than because you have to. Initially, this might sound great. If you google it, the internet is full of people who saved enough to achieve FIRE in their forties and, in a few cases, in their thirties.

My first reaction is to think that these smug-looking people must have made a huge amount by selling their business. However, this is not always the case. What they all seem to have in common is that they focused on extreme frugality to ensure that they saved at least 50% of everything they earned. This has a doubly positive effect. Because their outgoings are so low, they don't need a huge amount to cover them, which in turn leaves a good chunk of disposable income available to squirrel away.

Now for me this would *not* work as a motivator! I love my work and unemployment is definitely not one of my goals. More importantly, one of the reasons I love working is because it allows me to treat myself to lovely holidays and perhaps too many lunches out and Uber rides! A frugal life just wouldn't cut it for me.

But I do think there are some great lessons to be learned from these people:

1) They have very clear goals – they know financially what they want and by when they want to achieve it.

2) Their goal has a number attached to it, which in my experience means they are more likely to achieve it.

So What's My Ideal Budget?

In an ideal world you should be setting aside between 20% and 30% of your income into savings, investments, retirement planning and paying for insurances. However, for most people this isn't affordable. Especially at the start of your financial journey. Instead it is something to work towards each time you get a pay rise. Rather than absorbing the money into your daily expenditure, continue as if you never got it and increase the money you set aside into your short-, medium- or long-term savings. Try not to get bogged down in worrying whether this is 30% of your net/gross or annual pay. It will all be relative, but for the purpose of your budgeting, if you are working this out using a monthly income, it should be 30% of the money that you have after tax each month.

Remember: this is not going to be possible straight away for everyone and it definitely is not going to happen overnight. First you need to work out what is possible, realistic and doable. What is this figure for you? Write it in the box below.

> ....
>
> ....

What is this as a percentage of your take-home salary? Use this calculation to figure it out:

$$\frac{amount\ saved\ per\ month}{net\ income\ per\ month} \times 100$$

Write this figure in the box too. Your job going forward is to always be increasing this figure. For example, each time you get a pay rise you should save more.

So what are your goals? How much do you need per annum to live the life you want? Once you know this you can then work out what amount of money/assets you need to achieve your goals.

Hey, Big Spender

Whether you are a compulsive spender or just pay little regard to your spending habits, it all adds up to a lot. In David Bach's book *The Automatic Millionaire*, he talks about the importance of not wasting money. Of course, spend it on those things that make you happy (a holiday to Thailand, anyone?) but what about the small spends that all add up to drain the money from your account?

Bach talks about working out your 'latte factor'. This is working out (honestly) what you spend on the meaningless 'small stuff' and taking stock. It can often be these little spends that can do the most damage. I'd describe it as the 'Carrie Bradshaw realization' that the money she's spent on the shoes in her gorgeous walk-in wardrobe would have paid for a house deposit, but she's still living in a little rented apartment!

If we can cut down on short-term small spends, we can make some real gains when it comes to sticking to our budgets and meeting our long-term financial goals. If you love splashing the cash or get a real high every time you tap your contactless card, you might need to look at the real-world impact of your ad hoc spending. It's very exposing and a little bit addictive to examine the impact of what that 'one last drink' and a taxi home actually do to your financial goals.

To do this, keep a spending diary for at least two weeks and ideally for a whole month. I would recommend using a little notebook, but you can track it on your phone if you prefer this. You need to write down *everything*. This will give you a clear idea of where and when you are wasting money. Where do you spend most? What can you cut back on? Which of your priorities can you cut back on or do less of to really alter your spending? For example, I love getting my hair done, but instead of going every six weeks I go three times per year. This means I can continue to have the full salon experience without spending a fortune annually.

Questions to get in the habit of asking yourself:

- Do I need it?

- Will I be glad I bought it this time next year?

- Is it good value for money?

- Can I afford it?

How to Shop Around for Better Deals

There are many apps out there that help you to find a better deal than you might find on the high street for the same product. Invest some time searching through these and you might be able to claw back some cash on the items you need to purchase.

- **Too Good To Go:** This app links you in with restaurants in your area that would otherwise be throwing out food at the end of their day, and offers it at a massive discount.

- **ATM Hunter:** If you are like me and *hate* paying to use an ATM, this is the app for you. It uses your location to help you find your nearest free ATMs. Apparently free ATMs are becoming harder to find as banks close branches.

- **Voucher Apps:** There are loads out there so get in the habit of searching the discount apps before you purchase anything. Have a look at VoucherCodes, Vouchercloud or HotUKDeals. Groupon, LivingSocial and Wowcher are similar but they use group buying power to bag discounts.

- **Stocard:** Rather than carrying around all your loyalty cards, this app will store them on your phone so you never miss out on points again.

- **Cashback Apps:** These apps offer you cashback
  if you buy your purchase via their app. I have used
  this quite a lot for my toiletries shop and
  sometimes I manage to get a discount on the
  items I am looking out for at Christmas.

- **MySupermarket:** This app allows you to
  compare the cost of thousands of groceries
  from the main supermarkets. You fill your basket
  with the items you need and the app will tell you
  which supermarket is the cheapest and will place
  your order.

As well as using the above apps to cut your shopping
bill, don't be fooled into paying more for a product
that's packaged prettily whose plainer counterpart does
the exact same job. Known as 'pink tax', you'll find
products that are aimed at females tend to cost more,
without doing more. This happens on anything from
stationery, hygiene and sanitary products to razors and
even clothing.

Bagging a bargain?

The retail industry has been built on our inability to
leave a 'bargain' behind regardless of whether it looks
good or even fits – in financial behavioural economics
it's called 'anchoring'. If you believe something is worth
£100 and it is now on sale for £40, you feel that you are
saving £60. It is important to remember that a deal is
only a good deal if you were going to buy it anyway.

Before you fall into the trap, have a think: are you using the deal as a way to justify a purchase?

Reducing direct debits

Each year you need to make sure that you find a few hours to go through all of your direct debits to see if you need them still, if you can get them cheaper or if you can switch providers. My month to do this stuff is October and each year I have a success or two that makes it worthwhile.

Use the table overleaf to track your progress.

Here are my top tips:

- Research competitors' packages before calling up your provider to see if you can get a better deal from them.

- Always be prepared to leave and cancel the contract if it is a luxury. For example, last year I called my TV provider, Virgin, to see if I could get a better deal. They weren't able to give me one so I cancelled there and then. A few days later, they called offering me almost half price for a year if I came back.

- Sign up online to the Money Saving Expert Energy Club. You can set your own parameters and they will email you when you can get a better deal on your gas and electricity. I have set mine to alert me if I can save more than

Company	Monthly Cost	Keep/Cancel	Renegotiated?	New Monthly Cost

£50 per annum. It will also prompt you when you need to redo your gas and electricity deal once your fixed deal has expired. Ofgem have worked out that the average person could save £300 per annum just by switching provider!

- Adjust the thermostat. The Energy Trust has calculated that turning down your heating by one degree centigrade could save you £80–£90 per annum. Why not turn it down by two, wrap up in a jumper and save even more?

- Pay home insurance annually rather than monthly. By doing so you could probably save around 10% off the total annual cost.

- If you live alone, make sure you are getting the 25% discount that you are entitled to on your council tax.

- Turn off appliances that are on standby – this can apparently save you £50–£80 per annum!

Peer pressure and money

Keeping up with the Kardashians isn't a new thing, but with the dawn of social media has come even more pressure to acquire the latest 'must haves', whether it's an item of clothing, splashing at the salon on a new hair colour or owning the latest gadget. According to the

Guardian, nearly half of young people say they are forced into spending beyond their means, so if you are feeling this way, perhaps your friends are too. Don't be afraid to explain to them that you are on a budget, and get them in the game too if needs be. Perhaps seeing your financial focus will be what your friends need to motivate themselves. Say no to the cinema, but yes to a Netflix movie night with homemade popcorn; or rather than a meal out with friends, invite everyone round and get each person to be in charge of bringing a course or a side dish. How many clothes do you have in your wardrobe that are too small, too big, never worn or simply not loved? Rather than retail therapy, improve your financial wellbeing (and your Saturday-night outfits) by organizing a clothes swap party with friends and help to save the planet at the same time.

Food shopping

How much food do you waste? As a nation, we are terrible at it. Not only are we wasting food but we are also wasting a huge amount of money. According to the UK government we waste £12billion-worth of food a year. So can some of your cutting back come from preparing better when it comes to buying your groceries?

- Make a shopping list.

- Consider own brands.

- Do a meal plan – Love Food Hate Waste (a government-backed non-profit organization) has a two-week meal plan with downloadable shopping lists.

- The app Olio connects you with others in your local area to cut out food wastage by sharing unwanted ingredients for free.

Sweating the small stuff

Does your gym membership represent good value? Having a gym membership alone will not keep you fit and healthy if you rarely step through the front door. Be honest and if you aren't getting good value, cancel it and use the money for a new pair of trainers or a bike to motivate you to get outside. According to the *Mirror* newspaper, as a nation we are wasting £558million on gym memberships and 11% of memberships don't get used. Ouch.

Getting creative

- Sell clutter on eBay/local Facebook groups.

- Learn to say no – FOMO could be costing you a fortune!

- Think through a purchase before you buy. I love clothes and could shop online all day long. To force myself not to impulse buy, I put the things I want in the online basket and then wait a day or two before actually purchasing them.

- Think ahead and plan present-buying in the January and summer sales.

Sticking to Your Daily/Monthly Budget

Once you have your budget, how do you actually go about sticking to it? There are various ways, for example taking out the money you need for the week/day and not spending any more than this, or letting technology help you by having a pre-loaded cash card.

Whichever way you choose, you will need to know what your 'fun budget' is per month and make sure you stick to it. This would include all your spending on socializing, clothes, make-up or anything that is not strictly a necessity.

In order to resist temptation it's a good idea to separate your banking out. This is something you can easily achieve with online banking. Online banking will help you to set up sub-accounts to separate your money pots. If you log on to your bank account online (or via a banking app) you can label each account for each need (e.g. 'holiday' or 'annual'). This will help you to segment the money gradually throughout the year and to keep track of what is earmarked for what expenditure (keeping 'house deposit' separate from your 'hen do' account, etc.) rather than it all being muddled in one account. Here's an example of how this could work for you based on my own accounts:

- **Bank Account 1 – bills account:** This is where my husband and I contribute the same amount each month to cover all the essential outgoings (mortgage, gas/electricity, council tax, etc.). If you are living with housemates, the money you will pay out to cover bills and rent may need a direct debit setting up from this account into your 'house account', or to whoever's responsibility it is to pay the bills.

– **Bank Account 2 – my personal account:** This is where all the money I earn comes in and where I pay out to the bills account and fun account (see below). This is also where I pay for the outgoings that are just mine, e.g. mobile phone, gym, subscriptions/memberships and personal savings/investments. Monthly direct debits (and the standing orders to my savings accounts) are set up for the 1st of each month (i.e. the day I get paid).

– **Bank Account 3 – fun account:** This is the account for money earmarked for fun: clothes, meals out and ad hoc big purchases (e.g. replacing a laptop or phone). Once it's gone it's important not to siphon off money from your other accounts to pay for your fun. Being strict with yourself here will help you to develop the skills you need to build up strong financial foundations.

You may also want to have an annual savings account so that you can save monthly towards all your annual expenditure: car tax, MOT, contents insurance, Christmas and holidays, and so on. I like to have my savings out of sight so that I can't easily get access to them, so I have a separate savings account. To work out how much I should save monthly for annual expenses, I add up what they cost and divide the amount by twelve, e.g. Christmas is £1,000 which, divided by twelve, comes to £83.33. This is therefore the amount that I pay into my savings account each month by standing order. (I will be tackling savings and how to save in chapter 3.)

How to tally up outgoings – what should you count?

You should count everything! The only caveat to this is that I would recommend you don't get too hung up on cash withdrawals (unless you pay for a lot in cash). I don't bother working out what the cash I withdraw each week is spent on, I just make sure I take it from my fun account and it is within my allocated fun budget.

Sticking to your Budget Whilst on Holiday

There are many ways to save money when it comes to holidays so I have just included a few of the best ones in this section. The most important one for me is to be realistic about your budget. The five-star Instagram-worthy holiday is always going to be appealing, but if it derails your financial goals, is it really worth it? It is also important to remember that just because your friends are doing it doesn't mean you have to.

I know so many people who are paying for their bad financial behaviour in their twenties even a decade later. It is only now that the friend who was always on holiday and partying in the latest places is happy to admit that it was mostly paid for by credit card. The financial hangover from this spending lasts a lot longer than the fun of living in the moment, so it is important to have your holiday budget as realistic as possible. Being well prepared financially for a holiday should mean you don't derail your financial goals. Look at what you have put in your calendar or diary for the things you have committed to already, like weekend breaks, holidays or festivals, and fill in the table on p. 46.

Now consider the following:

- Have you forgotten to include any weekends away?

- If you look back at previous years, have you spent more or less than the figure you budgeted?

- With some clever planning in advance, would you be able to save (let's say 10%, for example) on the cost of your holiday? What could you do to have the same standard of holiday for less?

So now for my top holiday tips . . .

When	Where	How Long	Total Cost	Cost Per Month

Spending Money

- Credit cards can add a fortune on to your purchase in fees – 3% is not uncommon when abroad, so make sure you shop around for a card that doesn't charge you extra to make purchases abroad.

- Most credit cards will usually charge you if you use them to take cash out at an ATM so you need another way to be able to access cash. The solution I use is a pre-loaded foreign exchange card. They are really easy to use – just like a regular bank card. But you can pre-buy foreign currency and load it on to the card. Take a look at Revolut and FairFX – there are loads out there.

- When you are abroad, you may well be asked whether or not you want to pay in pounds or if you want to pay in local currency. At first glance, you might feel it is best to pay in pounds, but this is the wrong answer. According to the *Financial Times* Money section, 'pick the wrong one and you could pay nearly 8 per cent more'. The ability to pay in both is called dynamic currency conversion and is very common in Europe and Asia and I have often seen it in the USA. It is estimated that British tourists will pay nearly £500million in additional charges this year alone due to dynamic currency conversion. This extra money is split between the place you are spending money (e.g. hotel, restaurant, shop) and the company that they rent their payment terminals from.

Insurance

- Buy your insurance when you book a holiday and if you holiday more than once per year perhaps consider having an annual policy. Read the small print to make sure you have cancellation cover for your trip so if you can't go due to ill health you can get a refund.

- Have a European Health Insurance Card (EHIC) if you are travelling to Europe. This will allow you to get free or reduced cost healthcare. But it is no substitute for insurance – you do need both. There are loads of companies out there who will arrange an EHIC for you for a fee. You really don't need to pay for this service. They are so easy to apply for and they don't take long to come through.

Airport

- If you want to treat yourself, perhaps consider a lounge. If you book far enough in advance you can get access for as little as £20 and this will usually include food, drink and some newspapers/magazines. When I booked one recently we even got free fast-track passes through security, which was a nice surprise!

- Although you can't take drinks through security, you can take food. So if you are on a budget, taking a picnic with you can be a great way to save money. Some airports also have water fountains if you want to fill a bottle up once you are through security.

Flight Delays

- If your flight is delayed by more than two hours, you have a legal right to food, drink, to make a phone call and, if necessary, accommodation.

- If your flight arrives more than three hours late, then for short-haul flights you can claim around €250 and for long-haul flights this can be as much as €600 if it's more than four hours. Certain restrictions apply though. You have to have departed from an EU country or the airline you are travelling with needs to have a base in the EU.

Asking for a Pay Rise: How Much Will Really Make a Difference?

As the saying goes, 'every penny helps'. If you would like to see exactly how much extra a pay rise will give you in your pocket each month/week, just search online for a net pay calculator. There are loads of websites out there that will work this out for you, and it can be extremely useful to go in armed with this information when discussing a rise with your employers.

The real question, though, is not how much extra will you get, but what will you do differently with that extra money? Will you save/invest it or will you just spend it without any forethought? Your spending usually adjusts to suit your income. Therefore you need to make sure that from your first pay rise you don't get used to spending the extra money but instead put aside the difference straight away.

Another thing to be aware of is that you may want to negotiate a pay rise that focuses on an increase in benefits rather than actual cash – would a higher percentage into your pension actually improve your financial situation more than a pay rise? Perhaps a compromise of a bit of both?

If you are considering switching jobs for a higher salary, then it is also important to compare benefits that are being offered as well as the actual salary. Have you looked at what competitors are offering in terms of pensions, private medical insurance and sick pay?

One last thing: the gender pay gap is well documented and I think we owe it to ourselves (and society) to make sure we are being paid what we are worth and equal to 'the going rate', not just accepting the first offer on the table. Can you do some research and find out what your opposite-sex counterparts are being paid at your company? If you earn less, can you ask for an increase to match their salary?

Tidying Up Bank Accounts

It is easy to lose track of accounts if you have them dotted all over the place. Chances are, you may have had an old account for such a long time that it is not paying a great interest rate, for example a second current account you set up at university for emergency access to cash. To help, fill out the table overleaf to get your head around what accounts you have and where they are. If you want to keep an account, what new purpose will it be earmarked for?

If your accounts are all paying low interest rates, it is time to start researching the best accounts for you. You can find good advice in the money sections of the Sunday papers and on various money websites.

It is important to remember that the accounts need to be easy access. There's no point having one earmarked for an event happening next month if it has ninety days' notice to withdraw funds!

Finally, you should make this an annual job. Enter a recurring diary appointment to give yourself a nudge to do it.

Sorting Out Financial Paperwork

Clients arrive at my office with all sorts of financial filing 'systems'. The most common is paperwork thrown

Account	Amount In	Interest Rate	Keep or Close?	New Purpose
e.g. Lloyds	923	1%	Keep	Attending Jen's hen do

in a drawer or box as it comes through the post – usually still in the unopened envelope. This makes getting your hands on your paperwork extra hard!

Setting aside half a day (or maybe a full day if needs be) could well be the thing that helps to kickstart your financial plan.

Step-by-step Filing System

1) Get a shredder/scissors, in-tray, labels and filing cabinet/folder. Gather all paperwork that is lying around the house or is in inefficient filing systems.

2) Lay it all out on a table or floor, forming piles for each provider/bill/statement.

3) Shred anything that is not needed (or cut up into small strips if you don't have a shredder) and recycle any envelopes or leaflets that are generic. Remember that anything with your name/address and any other personal information should be shredded or cut up so no one can identify your details.

4) How long you should keep paperwork for depends on the paperwork in question. Use the table opposite to help you decide.

5) As your post arrives, immediately shred anything that you don't need to keep. The documents

Paperwork	How Long to Keep
Bank statements, credit card statements	Up to three months – but why not switch to online statements only?
Utility bills	A year
Warranties and receipts	Up to six years
Payslips	Keep all P60s and P45s. Keep all payslips until you receive your P60 for the year.
Medical information	Indefinitely
Personal information (e.g. birth certificate, will, marriage certificate, etc.)	For ever
Insurance documents	Until the policy ends
Loans/Mortgage statements	Until the debt is paid off or you change providers. When you change providers, you might like to keep the last statement for reference.
Business records for tax	Six years

you need to keep should go into the in-tray to await filing.

6) You need to have a section in the filing cabinet/folder for each financial item, e.g. Lloyds current account, contents insurance, gas and electricity, council tax, etc.

7) Each section should be clearly labelled so that you can easily see what goes where.

8) When it is time to file, the paperwork/ statement should be slotted in the front of each section so the newest is at the front.

9) Keep on top of it. I open my mail as it arrives and try to file weekly. Clearing out the back of each section takes place annually for me.

10) Finally, it's a good idea to keep a financial summary spreadsheet that you can update as you go along (see example on p. 190). As you work through this book, add in details of any assets (e.g. savings, investments and pensions) or debts (e.g. credit cards and loans) that you already have. As you pay down debt and build on your assets, make sure you keep your spreadsheet updated to keep you motivated.

Automating Your Finances

Given the choice, most people procrastinate. If you can take the choice out of your finances so that they take care of themselves with very little input from you, it leaves less room for bad financial decisions. A perfect example of this is a client of mine who trained to be an account-ant. When she got her first job, she was £40,000 in debt and her starting salary was £32,000. She was hugely dis-incentivized to start a financial plan because the debt just felt too much of a mountain to get over. Added to this was her anxiety about how to get on the property ladder. We put in place a plan that committed money to all the key areas of financial planning: debt, cash, invest-ments and retirement planning. At the beginning the focus was on the debt, then we moved to cash and then finally to investments and retirement planning. Because the plan happened automatically by direct debit each month, fast forward fifteen years (of good financial habits) and this client now has no debt (except for a manageable mortgage), an emergency cash buffer, a substantial invest-ment portfolio and a decent pension. The only action she needed to take was when she got a pay rise to remem-ber to up her monthly contributions.

Here are my three tops tips on how to automate your money:

1) Move your money the day you get paid –
   set up direct debits and standing orders to

your various sub-accounts so that this isn't a manual process. This will remove the need for you to remember and reduce the possibility of human error.

2) Set up direct debits to pay off any debt each month – this will avoid late fees and ideally you should be paying off the balance in full each month.

3) Set up direct debits to pay your bills monthly too, unless you get a decent discount for paying annually – this can often be the case with buildings and contents insurance.

Using technology to get ahead

For the techy ones amongst you, there are plenty of apps out there that can help you stay on top of your budget and track each spend as it goes out of your account.

– **Chip:** This is great if you find it hard to save each month. The app is free and is compatible with most UK bank accounts. It gathers information on your spending and uses the data to work out ways that you can save. Every couple of days it transfers an amount it has worked out to be affordable into a separate savings account.

– **Moneyhub, Money Dashboard and Yolt:** These apps bring all of your accounts into one place. It does cost to have the apps but this could be a very useful investment if you struggle to keep track of what you have where.

— **Moneybox:** This rounds up all your purchases and puts your money away into an investment stocks and shares ISA.

— **Squirrel:** This app segments your money into three groups – commitments, savings and spending – when you get paid and releases the money back to your current account bit by bit.

— **Savings Goals:** Helps you set goals and savings targets and tracks you as you work towards them. It will help you to understand whether you are on track or not.

— **Monzo:** This is gaining momentum as it combines budgeting features and spending breakdown into your banking. It comes with a card which you use exactly like a debit card and you can pre-load your account with your budget and get notifications each time you spend.

2

DEMOLISHING DEBT

Being in debt can have a huge impact on your wellbeing. Not having enough money can lead to feelings of isolation, or that you are not able to join in. It can lead to the deterioration of the relationships that you care about and sleepless nights caused by worry can lead to emotional stress. The link between mental health and debt problems is well documented and often a vicious circle is created. The more you are stressed out about debt, the more your mental health suffers and therefore the harder you find it to manage your money, which can lead to more debt.

Debt is not a new thing, of course, although the debt charity StepChange say that the number of young people seeking help for problem debts has been rising for many years. Two thirds of the people they helped in 2017 were under forty and 14% were under twenty-four. Of those under thirty-four, 70% regularly borrow to pay for household bills. Compared with the over-fifty-fives, millennials are more likely to have problems with their relationships and mental health problems caused by being in debt. Alarmingly, the *Financial Times* has even reported that 50% of twenty-five to thirty-four-year-olds have had trouble sleeping because they are worried about debt. All this is indicative of a big problem facing an entire generation.

When deciding to really tackle debt once and for all (not just yo-yoing between being in the black and then slipping back into old habits every couple of months), it's important to remember what you are doing it for. It's helpful to have this really clear in your mind so that if you notice you are starting to lose focus, you can remind yourself of the bigger picture:

1) How will you feel when you are debt free?

2) What will being debt free help you to achieve that you currently are not?

3) What will you think about when you no longer have to worry about debt again?

Write the answers to these questions here:

1) ....

....

2) ....

....

3) ....

Why Do We Get Into Debt?

Credit is so easy to get your hands on these days and it has become an acceptable part of the way we live. I often come across people who have borrowed to pay for things such as a wedding, a holiday, an outfit and especially general day-to-day spending. As a society we are living beyond our means and racking up debt after debt.

Debt also commonly occurs at times of financial concern, e.g. divorce, unemployment, ill health, etc. On top of this, government policy around benefits and the banking sector as a whole can make these situations even worse. The debt then compounds the severity of the situation and magnifies the stress.

Most debt is bad because you are paying interest for instant gratification. The only thing I can think of that is an exception to this rule is a mortgage. Very few people can afford to buy a house without a mortgage, and a house (usually) goes up in value.

Types of Debt

It is important to get your head around all the different types of debt that are out there, in order to identify the right strategy to help you clear this debt.

Overdrafts

An overdraft is a very common debt, mainly because they are part of your current account and so it is easy to stray into unless you are careful with your money management.

Over 40% of eighteen to thirty-five-year-olds don't know what interest they are paying on their overdraft. This is concerning because an overdraft is often a very expensive way to borrow money, especially if it is unauthorized – i.e. not pre-agreed with the bank.

An overdraft is also mentally disregarded when people think about debt. They think about their bank balance at the beginning of the month when actually the reality is how much you owe the day before you get paid.

Overdrafts are typically charged per day that you use them and/or an interest charge too. So when you are filling out your debt table on p. 74, make sure you don't forget to add your overdraft and perhaps also work out what your typical charge is per month so you can rank it in terms of cost in comparison to other debts.

Credit Cards

Credit cards can play a positive role in financial planning or they can be our downfall. I use two credit cards each month as part of our financial strategy. My fun money goes on to my credit card and the debt is cleared in full each month; our joint spending, e.g. supermarket, kids' clothes and holidays, all goes on a separate credit card and again is paid off in full each month. Both cards improve our long-term finances in that they accrue air miles and free flights, which we then use to pay towards our holidays.

It is vital that you get into the habit of clearing your credit card each month to avoid paying interest. The easiest way to do this is to automate it. You need to set up a direct debit with your credit card company to clear your card each month from your current account. Failing to do this means the money that rolls over to the next month incurs interest and so costs you more. Most credit cards are then set up so that when you pay off some money on the credit cards the next month, it clears the cheapest debt first, i.e. it will clear the newest purchases first that aren't yet incurring interest. The debt from the previous month will then roll over and incur even more interest in the following month, and so on. According to the Money Advice Service, the average credit card debt per household is £2,294. If you only made the minimum repayments each month, it would take more than twenty-five years to pay off this debt.

So if you know you are not going to be able to clear the credit card in full and will therefore incur interest, you need to look for a 0% credit card. Look carefully into the terms and conditions of the card because it differs per provider. You can get 0% on balance transfers, for example, but still be charged interest if you continue to spend on the card.

Remember, the credit card companies aren't offering

you the 0% because they are kind, they do so to tempt you to move to them and then stay with them once the free interest period ends – and you are hit with high interest rates. So make sure you add a reminder to your phone's calendar a month before the 0% period ends to ensure that you switch to another 0% if you haven't already been able to clear the debt in full.

Student Loans

It feels like student loans are always hitting the headlines and the press are frequently citing £50,000 as the amount that the average person is going to be in debt after university. This isn't strictly true. There is a lot of false information out there and this false information is driving people's decisions as to whether or not to go to university – therefore potentially taking you on a different path in life. So let's talk through the myths and work out what is fact and what is fiction.

You can apply for a tuition loan (maximum £9,250 per annum) and also a maintenance loan. The maintenance loan is there to help you pay towards your living costs. The maintenance loan was announced in 2015 and has replaced the maintenance grant. The amount you can borrow depends on where you live/study and also your household income. The maximum you can be eligible to borrow is £11,354 in 2018/19.

What you pay back and how quickly you pay it back

depends on what you earn and by how much your pay increases. Currently, you start paying back the loan only once you are earning more than £25,000 per annum, and you pay 9% of everything that you earn above this threshold. If you haven't paid off your loan within thirty years, the debt is written off.

Repayments are made automatically through the tax system and stop when your student loan is fully paid off. Even if you move abroad, you will still need to pay but the government will work out how much you need to repay once you have submitted an Overseas Income Assessment Form.

If you are self-employed, HMRC will calculate how much you owe based on the tax returns that you submit.

When is my loan wiped?

Student loans are wiped if you have not paid them off after a certain period of time. Again, this depends when you took out your loan.

If you are unsure about what loan you have, you can contact the Student Loans Company or take their online test which will take you through a decision tree to reveal which loan you have.

How much do I owe?

So what is your situation? Dig out a recent statement (or give the Student Loans Company a call) and find out how much you owe and the terms of your payment

What rate do I pay?

	Date	Interest Rate
Pre 2012	1 September 2018–19	1.75%
Post 2012	1 September 2017– August 2018	Either RPI[1] plus 3% or RPI plus 3.3%

[1] RPI is the Retail Price Index, a measure of inflation.

Start Date	Age When Wiped
1990–97 (under age forty)	Either twenty-five years after the first payment of your last loan (usually the start of your last year) or when you reach age fifty.
1990–97 (aged forty+)	When you reach age sixty.
1998–2005	When you reach age sixty-five.
2006–11	Twenty-five years from the first April after graduation.
2007–11 (Scottish residents)	Twenty-five years from the first April after graduation.
2012+	England and Wales: thirty years from the first April after graduation. Scotland: thirty-five years from the first April of graduation. NI: twenty-five years from the first April after graduation.

[Source: Money Saving Expert]

plan. Record it here so you can add this to the debt table on p. 74.

Should I pay off my loan early?

This really depends on if you will definitely have it all paid off or not in time. If you were to reach the point when your loan is wiped, still owing, overpaying would have been pointless. So because this is quite difficult to predict and calculate, if you are in a position to overpay but aren't doing all the positive financial things we have already discussed in this book, I would suggest you focus on making these financial changes first, instead of over-paying on your student loan.

One final thought: don't be afraid to face your student loan head on – you might even find that the Student Loans Company owes you! A few years ago, I looked at a client's payslip and noticed she was still paying her student loan, which seemed strange. She agreed and gave them a call and our hunch was right – she had been overpaying and she claimed a refund of over £1,000 back. So how does this happen? The Student Loans Company only finds out how much you have paid back once per year from HMRC. As a result, you could still be paying when in fact you have cleared it. The SLC will write to you to let you know if you have overpaid, but this can take an age to work its way through the system. If you think you may have overpaid, you can give the SLC a call and they will ask you to provide evidence. Useful evidence will be your last SLC statement and also your payslip, which shows what you have been paying back each month.

Family Loans

Often loans from family members get ignored because they are borrowed on a much more flexible basis than, say, a loan from a bank. However, the emotional ties that come with this type of loan make it a very important topic for me to address. These loans should be taken as seriously as you would a bank loan, even if you feel the person has allowed you to borrow the money on a flexible basis. Keeping the loan as a professional agreement will mean that the kind gesture will not get in the way of your familial relationship or friendship. Before you take a loan from a person that is close to you, make sure you discuss what is acceptable and what is not:

- How much should you pay back and when?

- When will the debt be cleared?

- What interest is being paid, if any; how much and what would happen to this interest if, for example, the Bank of England base rate went up or down?

- What if you have difficulty in paying? How would this impact their lifestyle and plans?

If you already have a loan from a family member and you haven't discussed these questions, now would be a good time to figure out what you still owe and to set up a repayment agreement that works for both of you.

Assets 'On Finance'

Something that costs you more than it makes you is not an asset! The most common one I see is a car. But I have seen the weird and wonderful on credit too. In my early career I met a couple who had three hoovers on credit simultaneously. Buying things on credit should be avoided at all times. The only exception to this rule that I can think of is if it is something you were going to buy anyway and it is interest free for the entire repayment period.

Getting On Top of Debt

Here are five steps to help you get a head start when it comes to identifying and paying off your debt:

1) To get on top of your debt, start by filling
   in the following debt table. Don't guess the
   amounts and interest you are paying – call up
   the providers for accurate details if you are
   unsure.

2) Now adjust the budget planner you filled in at
   the beginning of the book on p. 25 – you need
   to make sure you are throwing as much money
   as possible from your monthly income towards
   clearing your debt. Make sure you cut back on
   anything remotely extravagant to get this debt
   cleared as quickly as possible. Remember the
   cutting-back tips in chapter 1 – can you
   implement any of these to free up the extra
   money to clear your debt?

3) This might sound illogical, but you need to
   build up a mini 'slush fund' or emergency cash
   buffer. The reason you are in debt is probably
   because you have never had an emergency cash
   buffer, so if things go wrong or you need a
   chunk of money unexpectedly, you have had
   to rely on debt. If you are focusing on paying
   down your debt and then hit a bump in the
   road, you will have no choice but to go back to
   relying on debt again, but if you have a small
   slush fund of say £500–£1,000 then you can fall
   back on this rather than debt.

Who I Owe	How Much I Owe	Interest Rate	Minimum Payment

4) There are two schools of thought when it comes to paying down debt. The first is the most logical one, and the second is a way to help keep you motivated to ensure that you stay focused on clearing the debt. In either case, you need to make sure you keep paying the minimum payments you owe on all your debt. Option one is that you pay down the debt of the most expensive loan/credit card first and focus all your energy on this. Once it is cleared you then throw everything you can at the next most expensive debt. Option two is to pay the smallest debt off first and then focus on the second smallest debt, and so on. The reason behind this method is that the small wins early on are designed to keep you focused and on track at the time when you are most likely to stray, i.e. before it becomes a habit and before there is light at the end of the tunnel. So which option will you choose? Whichever one it is, make sure you stick with it and divert all the money you were paying into the first debt straight into the second once the first is paid off. This will lead to the debt cutting down as quickly as possible. If you get a pay rise, divert the extra money to the debt too.

5) Stay focused – remember at the beginning of the chapter how you said you would feel when

your debt is cleared and how your life will change once it is? Hold this in mind over time and, if you have a little wobble, try to remember that you are working towards a greater good in the long term!

Supporting Yourself When in Debt

There are many things you can do to support yourself out of debt. Getting to know yourself better is the first step to becoming your own personal debt counsellor. What are your key triggers to spending? If you're not sure, start a journal to track your daily spending and also note how you felt. Are these feelings different when you spend money that isn't yours (credit cards, overdrafts, etc.) compared to when the money is your own? Are there any tricks that you can play on yourself to curb the spending? I have a friend who used to go clothes shopping when she fell out with people, had a bad day at work or had a relationship split. She learned to manage her impulse to shop by doing fake online shopping. She would plan outfits, make wish lists and go through the whole online process right up to the point of checking out, stopping just before she actually had to pay for the items.

If you are an impulse spender, the simplest solution is don't take your cards out with you, just withdraw a sensible amount of cash to get by with. This will avoid temptation and help you to realize what you actually need versus what you would like in an ideal world. Or how about only allowing yourself to purchase on a certain day of the month? This will help you to take time and to consider if you really need it.

If you know you are an ostrich when it comes to money, perhaps you can turn this into one of your strengths? For example, I have a client who in the past has been a real head-in-the-sand sort of person when it comes to money. This had a huge impact on her in her twenties and thirties and it was only in her forties that she realized what works for her is to ignore money for six days a week, but on Thursdays she has to tackle any money issues which have arisen that week. She also has to open all her mail, update her financial plan and look at her budget on this day.

Once you have got your head around how to support yourself, perhaps you can start to build yourself a support network? We all know the old adage 'a problem shared is a problem halved'. Is there a person who you can trust to talk through your situation with? Perhaps it is a friend or a family member, or if you need someone less personally connected to you, a professional, like your doctor. Could you set up a 'getting out of debt' club with a friend? You could be each other's budgeting buddy. This will help you both be accountable to each other for your spending, plus you can help to motivate each other along the way. If those closest to you are also focused on being money savvy, this will help to reduce peer pressure to spend too.

What could you do that is positive instead of turning to spending? Invite your friend over for a coffee and catch-up rather than meeting at the pub? Set yourself a physical challenge like going for a run every Saturday? Research free fun days out?

If you have tried these measures and you are still struggling to tackle your debt, perhaps it is time to consider if you need professional support. If you have had a bad experience in the past with, say, a bank, try to put this aside. It doesn't mean that the next professional will not be helpful. A good indication that you are out of your depth where your debt is concerned is if you are struggling to meet your minimum payments each month or your debts are bigger than your annual income. If you fall into these categories then you might find the organizations listed in the back of this book helpful (see Resources on p. 249) as they can offer you personal advice for your unique circumstances.

Debt Jargon Buster

When it comes to facing debt, one thing that can add to our stress is all the jargon lenders use when talking about what you owe. Here's a handy list of the key terms and what they mean, to help you face the debt head on:

APR: This stands for Annual Percentage Rate, a set way of working out the cost of a loan or debt. It takes into account the interest you are paying and also any other charges. The higher the APR, the more you are paying.

Arrears: This is where you still owe money that is overdue, i.e. you didn't pay back a debt on time.

Bankruptcy: A legal proceeding when you are unable to repay your debts. It shares your assets between the companies that you owe the money to and lets you make a debt-free fresh start. This fresh start does come with restrictions though. The bankruptcy will stay on your credit file for six years.

CCJ: County Court Judgement – a type of court order that can be registered against you if you fail to repay a debt that you owe. A CCJ will negatively impact your ability to get credit in the future.

Consolidation Loan: If you have debts across several cards/loans, you can take out a single loan to clear them all. Some people like to do this as it simplifies their debt, putting it all in one place with one monthly payment.

Credit: Credit always sounds like a bad word, but don't forget that if your account is in credit it means you have money that is available to spend. This is always useful to remember when you receive your (often confusing) energy bill. If you have bought something on credit, this is a debt. This means that a credit card/lender has effectively paid for it for you and you need to pay them back.

Credit Card: A payment card that allows the cardholder to pay for goods/services. You don't have to pay for these things immediately and will be sent a monthly bill to pay for all the things that you have bought. If you don't pay the balance off in full on time, you will have to pay interest on the amount you have borrowed (unless you have a 0% interest credit card).

Credit Report: This gathers together all the information stored about you with a credit agency. It is what lenders will look at to decide whether or not you are credit-worthy.

Debit: Money that is taken from an account.

Debit Card: A card that you can use to purchase things. This card replaces cash and whatever you spend is taken automatically from your account.

Debt Management Plan: This may be put in place if you have debt that you can't afford in order to pay creditors a small amount each month or if you can't afford to pay right now but you can in a few months' time. A debt management team usually sits between you and the creditor and will often charge you a fee for this.

Hire Purchase Agreement: A credit agreement that allows you to pay for goods in instalments. You don't own the goods until the last instalment has been paid. Cars are often purchased in this way.

Overdraft: If you have spent more money than you have in your current account, sometimes the bank will offer you an overdraft facility. This is money the bank is willing to lend to you flexibly over the short term (an authorized overdraft). If you have an unauthorized overdraft, this is where either you don't have your bank's permission to borrow or you are borrowing more than your authorized overdraft. Be aware that overdrafts can often be an expensive way to borrow.

Refinancing: This is where you set up a new loan to replace existing debt.

Secured Loan: Borrowed money that is secured against (usually) a property. If the debt is not paid off, the lender may take the property and sell it to recoup the debt.

Store Card: A credit card, but which only allows you to purchase things from one particular shop.

Subprime Lending: Lenders who are willing to lend to people who wouldn't be able to get credit (loans/credit cards) from mainstream lenders because they have a poor credit rating.

3
CASH SAVINGS

These days, cash is no longer king. Cash in the bank is not beating inflation (inflation is when prices rise over time – for example, can you remember when Polos were 10p and now they are 65p?) and therefore is not working for you, let alone working hard. Gone are the days of 5% cash rates; 1% is now a 'good' rate. As a consequence of this, you don't want to keep too much in cash, and for the cash you do have you need to make sure you are getting the best rate that you can.

How to Save – Adjusting Your Mindset

Saving should not be about saving what's left over at the end of each month because chances are there won't always be anything left over. Just as we spend more if we earn more, it is possible to adjust our spending down to suit our budget. Do you remember a time when you earned less? How has your lifestyle changed since then? Are you any happier now than you were then? It is important to adjust your mindset so that you are thinking of saving as an essential outgoing, rather than a nice afterthought.

Get your head around what money does to you emotionally. The high of that retail therapy session doesn't last long and I like to remind myself of this, especially when I'm taking what once felt like a 'must have' item along to the charity shop. The financial coach Simonne Gnessen wrote that 'saving is a way of prioritizing your future self'. I love this sentiment.

How Much Should You Save?

This is a very personal question. It depends on your outgoings, your goals and your personal situation. As standard you should aim to have six months' worth of outgoings in cash at all times. This is your emergency cash buffer. If you have a family, a large mortgage and irregular income, you might prefer to have more. If you are young, free and single, then perhaps you can get away with less (three months).

On top of this you then need to consider what you need money for in the next five years, e.g. a new car, a special holiday or even something huge like a house deposit. Work out what these cost and add this to your emergency cash buffer goal.

This always seems scary in the early days, so don't worry if you don't have anywhere near to this amount. But if you don't know what you need, you will be less focused when it comes to achieving it.

When it comes to building up your emergency cash buffer, you need to commit to an amount that you are going to set aside each time you get paid and forget about it (until there is an emergency). It is important to set yourself clear boundaries on what you can or cannot use your cash buffer for, e.g. yes to a new boiler in the middle of winter, but no to a last-minute holiday to Ibiza! This emergency cash buffer will be the backbone of your financial plan and once this is achieved you can start to work towards the other areas that are important.

If you have more than you need in cash, then you should ask yourself why. You potentially have too much in an asset that is not keeping pace with inflation. Perhaps you should be starting to consider if investing is right for you. (More on this in chapter 9.)

What is a Good Savings Rate?

An ideal savings rate is one that beats inflation, but that just isn't possible when it comes to easy access savings accounts at the moment.

So what is inflation currently? There are two broad measures of the rate of increase of prices over time. These are the Retail Price Index (RPI) and the Consumer Price Index (CPI). RPI is currently 3.5% and CPI is 2.4%. The difference between RPI and CPI is that they include slightly different things when they are measuring the change in price over a year. RPI includes the cost of housing (e.g. council tax and mortgage interest) whilst CPI doesn't. Try to keep up to date with the change in inflation over time as this will help you form a current view on what you would need from your emergency cash account to beat it.

Currently (and it has been this way for quite a few years now), cash savings rates have been around the 1% mark. If your savings are sitting in accounts that you have had for ages, you could find they are paying very low rates of return (e.g. 0.1–0.2%). To get the best accounts you need to shop around – you will find the internet a great place to start your research and also the Sunday newspapers. Both sources will be kept up to date regularly and you may find that you need to split up your cash buffer into separate accounts to get the best rates. For example, at the moment the best instant access savings rates have maximum allowable balances of a few thousand pounds in total, so you may need another account if you plan on putting in more than the limit in order to reap the rate benefits.

Remember, the account needs to be easy access so that you can access it in an emergency, so don't be tempted by fixed accounts that will lock your money up for, say, ninety days or a year. Put it in your diary to check your savings rates at the end of the tax year (March) and mid-way through the year (September).

To ISA or Not to ISA

It used to be that interest on cash savings was automatically taxed at 20% by the bank and then if you were a high or additional rate tax payer you had to file the amount in your tax return where the rest of the tax that you owed was paid (an additional 20% or 25%). That is why ISAs were popular. Any cash in an ISA (Individual Savings Account) would be protected from tax on the interest.

However, things changed on 6 April 2016 when the government introduced the Personal Savings Allowance. Basic rate tax payers are now allowed to each earn £1,000 of savings income before any tax is paid. Higher rate tax payers can earn up to £500 and additional rate tax payers don't have an entitlement. If your taxable income is less than £17,500, then you don't pay any tax on your savings at all.

You don't need to do anything to claim your personal allowance. You should carry on doing a self-assessment as normal if you are required to do so. You will need to do a tax return if any of the following apply to you in the last tax year:

- You had a self-employed income of more than £1,000.

Make it Serve You – 'F*ck You' Money

It is always best to negotiate from a position of strength. I first read about the term '"F*ck You" Money' in a business book so I can't claim it as my own, but it is a very important concept to think about. Money should give you security, choices and opportunities.

Consider the following:

- How much easier would it be to ask for a pay rise if you had £20,000 in the bank and didn't 'need' the money but it was about getting what you were actually worth?

- How much easier would it be to ask your boss for a short sabbatical if you had a year's worth of cash in the bank so if they said no you knew you could just go anyway and still have time to get a new job when you got back?

- How much easier would it be to quit your job and set up your own business if you had financial security?

When I had just finished university I was working in a job where I didn't have a clue what I was doing and I was just making it up as I went along. Going to work on a Monday was a huge chore – I definitely was not living the career dream that I had planned. At the same time, two university friends of mine were plotting to go travelling and I wanted in. I wasn't sure how it was possible and then my grandma gave me £2,100 for my twenty-first birthday and my mum and dad agreed to buy my round-the-world ticket. We planned to go in six months' time! This gave me a new perspective on my job. Mondays suddenly weren't a chore because I knew that I had a way out and the purpose of working was to save enough so I could take a year off. Although some of the money was given to me, it was my first exposure to '"F*ck You" Money'. From then on I promised myself I would always have some money squirrelled away so I could make brave life choices rather than chugging along day to day.

So should you have some '"F*ck You" Money' in your savings pot? If so, how much? When you consider '"F*ck You" Money', what brave things would you plan? Are these things in your financial goals at the beginning of the book? If not, why not? Add these to your goals list to make them happen!

- Your income from savings and investments or dividends from shares was £10,000 gross or more.

- You got more than £2,500 from renting out property (there is a helpline you can call if you earn between £1,000 and £2,500: tel. 0300 200 3300).

- You made a profit from selling an investment or, say, a second home.

- You are a company director.

- Your income was over £50,000 and you or your partner claim child benefit.

- You had income from abroad.

- You lived abroad and had UK income.

- Your taxable income was over £100,000.

- HMRC wrote to you saying you didn't pay enough tax – they sent you a P800.

- Your state pension was more than the personal allowance.

- You'd like to pay Class 2 National Insurance.

(Source: www.gov.uk)

Banks now pay all savings interest without tax and they will provide HMRC with all the information on accounts that are in sole names. If you are a joint account holder and not in the self-assessment system then you should contact HMRC to report the savings.

Premium Bonds – An Alternative to Cash?

A Premium Bond is like a ticket in a lottery where you can win various cash prizes, the biggest being a million pounds. The lottery is drawn monthly and if you don't win, your ticket is re-entered into next month's draw.

The downside is that if you never win, your money never grows and so it is eroded by inflation. Now this is exactly the problem that I have. I must be the unluckiest Premium Bond holder in the UK. As a child I was given them on an ad hoc basis from about the age of seven, and I have been paying in religiously every month since I was twenty-five. And I have *never* won!

I am still, however, paying into Premium Bonds monthly. The reason I am doing this is because cash rates are so low at the moment, I don't feel I am giving up much in terms of interest but the gambler in me loves the small chance that I might win a million.

I regularly get people asking me how Premium Bonds work and whether they are the right thing to save into or not, so here is a handy overview:

- Two people win £1million each month – there's a 1 in 35,000,000,000 chance of this happening per ticket. The smallest prize each month is £25 and the chance of winning something with each £1 ticket is 24,500 to 1.

- You can check on the Premium Bond website to see if you have won. You can also see who has won each month and how much they had invested – this is a guilty pleasure for me!

- The annual average return is now 1.4%.

- The minimum investment is £100.

- You can withdraw your money without notice or penalty.

- Winnings are exactly that and so are tax free.

- The maximum you can now have in Premium Bonds is £50,000 per person.

- The computer that generates the numbers is still called Ernie and this stands for Electronic Random Number Indicator Equipment.

So are they worth it? Obviously that depends if you win or not! As the winnings are tax free this is more appealing the more tax you pay. It is especially appealing to people who pay 45% tax (i.e. earn over £150,000) as they do not get a savings allowance, which means they must pay tax on all of their savings.

I am sticking with mine for now, but when returns on savings accounts start to improve I will stop paying in monthly and switch my monthly direct debit to topping up my cash savings.

So do you have any Premium Bonds? Perhaps you do, but your parents/relatives have just never handed them over. It may be worth checking and if you still have the paper versions, you might find it useful to switch to the online account to help you keep track. That way you will be alerted if you win and prizes will be paid out automatically back into your account to buy more bonds or, if you have requested it, to your bank account.

Now when I say 'it may be worth checking', it really might – there are so many people who have won prizes that are waiting to be collected and there are even prizes worth up to £100,000 each that are yet to be claimed!

Savings Jargon Buster

AER: Annual Equivalent Rate – shows you what the interest rate would be if it was paid for a full year. It allows you to compare different savings rates. The higher the rate, the better for you.

Bonus Account: An account that opens with an additional bonus rate of interest for a stated period of time.

Easy Access Account: These accounts allow you to withdraw your money when you need it without restrictions.

Faster Payment Service: A payment system which allows you to transfer up to £100,000 and aims to be made the same day if instructed before 8 p.m.

Fixed Rate Savings Account: The interest rate that is paid is fixed and therefore won't change for a set period of time.

Gross Interest: The amount of interest that is paid before tax is deducted.

Interest Rate: The money paid to you for depositing money with a bank/savings account. It is usually expressed as a percentage.

ISA: Individual Savings Account – the interest on these savings accounts is not taxed by the government. The amount you can pay in is set by the government each tax year and it runs from 6 April one year to 5 April the next.

Junior ISA: Introduced in 2011. It is the parent's responsibility to open an account unless the child is over sixteen. They are available to those under eighteen and you can have cash versions or stocks and shares versions.

Maturity: With regard to savings, this is when an account will reach the end of its fixed term.

Notice Account: An account where you have to give notice to access your money. For example, with a ninety-day notice account, you can't touch the money for ninety days after asking to withdraw without penalty.

Personal Savings Allowance: The amount of interest you are allowed to earn before you pay tax on savings. The amount you are allowed depends on whether you are a basic, high or additional rate tax payer.

Variable Interest: The rate of interest that you get on your savings account varies over time, usually dictated (but not always) by the Bank of England base rate.

4
GETTING ON THE LADDER

Buying a house has become a British obsession! The early 2000s brought property price chat to the dinner-party table and overnight everyone seemed to become a buy-to-let landlord. It is important to remember that in a lot of countries property ownership is not such an essential thing. Germany, for example, is a nation of renters and they are at the bottom of the list of European home-owners with just 46% of households owning the home they live in.

So the first thing to work out is: why do you want to buy? What's important to you and what will make you happy and support your lifestyle rather than impede it? There is no point being holed up in a shoebox if it saps all your money and leaves nothing disposable for your hobbies, holidays or whatever is important to you. Looking back to the goals spreadsheet that you filled out at the beginning of this book, did you set any goals for property buying?

Write your reasons here for wanting to buy:

Setting Your Buying Goals

Now you know *why* you want to buy, think: *where* are you going to buy? Are you setting your sights too high? Does your ideal now (zone one party flat in London) fit in with your medium- and long-term plans? In a perfect world we would buy a flat in the right part of town not long after we begin our first job and then buy the forever home when we are ready to settle down. However, years of property prices spiralling out of control and wages not keeping up have led to the average first-time buyer age being thirty and needing to have a deposit of £20,622.

It's a good idea, therefore, to think past the 'ideal first flat' stage if you can. Purchasing a flat and then a forever home would lead you to paying two lots of stamp duty, solicitors' fees, moving costs and also two lots of the hassle that comes with moving!

So could you rethink your goals in order to buy for keeps?

Here are the questions to consider:

1) Do you imagine that you will always live in the area/town that you are living in now?

2) Have you done your research (e.g. Rightmove and Zoopla?) followed by actually looking round the types of places you would like to buy?

3) Is where you will end up cheaper than where you are planning to live in the short term?

4) If you bought your ideal first-time property, is it future-proofed? For example, if you intend to have kids, could it become a family home? Are the schools good in the area?

5) If you could afford a place with an extra bedroom, could you rent it out to a friend in the short term to help make ends meet and then have it all for yourself/for a family in the future?

6) Are there any other areas you could consider that might be cheaper that aren't immediately obvious?

7) What deposit will you need? How long will it take you to save? What do you need to be

earning to be able to get the mortgage you will need? Speak to a mortgage broker to get an idea of whether your income stacks up, and if not, how much extra you need to be working towards in order to buy.

8) When do you want to retire/be mortgage free?

Write your buying goals here:

Getting Your Finances in Tip-top Condition to Buy

Like all of the financial planning we have covered so far, the key to achieving your goals lies in taking small steps towards meeting them, and identifying any barriers that could get in your way. In order to buy a home you need to consider a great deal of things – your deposit, the available mortgage rates, etc. – but did you know that you also really need to think about your credit score?

Since the credit crunch, the industry has redefined

the rules regarding affordability and what you can borrow. In the months/years in the lead-up to buying you need to be able to show a lender that you are a sensible borrower. These are the sort of things lenders will be looking at:

- Have debt under control and ideally cleared by the time you come to get a mortgage (don't panic about student loans though as not all lenders will take them into account).

- Don't be living in your overdraft.

- Erratic spending – this will freak out some lenders.

- Whether you have a regular income and a stable job (3–6 months minimum). If you are looking to move jobs, it might make sense to wait until you have sorted out your mortgage, or to delay your purchase/remortgage until you have settled into your new role.

- Have as big a deposit as possible.

- Have all your paperwork in order so you can easily get things to your lender or broker quickly when they ask for it.

- If you are self-employed you need to get up-to-date with your tax returns and get an SA302 from your accountant in preparation. An

SA302 is a brief summary report of the income that has been reported to HMRC.

How to Clean Up Your Credit Score

- Register to vote – being on the electoral roll is an easy way to boost your credit rating. Make sure this matches your address too for all other things.

- Pay your bills on time – you can automate this by setting up direct debits for the day/day after you get paid.

- Check there aren't any mistakes on your credit report – there are plenty of websites that offer this service (see the Resources section, p. 250). Your address may be slightly wrong, for example, or your date of birth.

- Do you have any financial association with another person with a poor rating? A good example of this could be a joint account with an old housemate who has a poor credit rating. You can check this by looking at your credit file and then writing to the credit reference agency to ask for a notice of disassociation once you have closed the account.

- Check for fraudulent activity on your credit report. Perhaps someone has fraudulently applied for credit in your name? If so, contact the credit reference agency immediately.

- Moving house too often can make some lenders feel uncomfortable.

- Cancel unused store and credit cards – they make lenders nervous as they know you have the ability to go into debt, but no evidence of how much and whether you will be paying it off on time.

How to Report or Fix Mistakes on Your Credit File

Challenge any inaccuracies, reporting the mistake to the credit reference agency. They have twenty-eight days to remove the information or to tell you why they don't believe you are right. During this time frame the mistake will be marked as disputed and lenders aren't allowed to rely on this information when assessing your credit rating.

Also, speak directly to the lender that you believe has made the mistake on your file.

Did you know that you can add a notice of correction to your credit report if the information on the report no longer represents your situation? For example, say you missed payments whilst you were out of work but now you are in a stable job again, you can add this information. They give you up to 200 words to explain your situation.

Get Renting to Help Your Credit Score: Rental Exchange Scheme

If you pay rent on time (every time) then you could use this record to boost your credit rating. The Rental Exchange scheme records your rental payments and sends the results to the credit reference agency Experian.

The Rental Exchange scheme was launched in 2016. The way it works is that you pay your rent to a third party called Credit Ladder and then Credit Ladder passes the money on to your landlord and informs Experian that you have paid on time.

You will need to get your landlord's permission and you must be a private tenant. Most lenders at the moment don't take the rental payments into account directly, but over time the regular payments should improve your ability to get a mortgage because your Experian score will improve.

Finally, a good habit to get into is to check your credit report every twelve to eighteen months to make sure it is accurate.

How Will I Ever Get a Deposit Together?

There is no instant fix to getting a deposit together other than making short-term sacrifices. I decided that I was happy to make big short-term sacrifices to ensure that I got my deposit together as quickly as possible for my first flat. I did this by working in a bar (as a tequila girl) and a restaurant in the evenings and at the weekends, on top of my trainee financial adviser day job. It meant that I had to turn down holidays and take packed lunches to work. I also lived with my now in-laws which I am sure was more of a chore for them! However, this really did mean that almost everything I earned could be saved and I had my deposit together in just over a year.

If you are not keen on the more inhibiting short-term saving strategy that I adopted and feel these sacrifices are a step too far, the most important thing you have to do is make sure that you stay motivated. It will be imperative to remind yourself regularly why you are doing what you are doing so the lure of spending that money on something else doesn't become irresistible! Temptations are always going to crop up, but that is exactly what they are . . . temptations. They need to be avoided by imagining how you will feel when you first put your key in your own front door.

I also don't want to sugar-coat the truth though: with property prices rising faster than people can save the deposit, taking your time is going to cost you more and more money, so sorting out your deposit saving strategy and considering the compromises you need to make in earnest should be a real priority.

You have to learn to know when you are telling yourself lies, too. So many people tell me they are saving for a house. 'How much are you saving?' I ask. '£500 per month,' they say. 'So how much have you got in total?' I ask. '£400,' they reply. 'OH!' I think to myself. This is a perfect example of how people convince themselves they are saving, but conveniently forget they are also drawing money out from this pot at the end of the month when their credit card bill arrives.

Here are some ways that might work for you when looking to save up that deposit, and a rundown of the savings and help-to-buy schemes available.

Get Budgeting Again!

How much do you need to save each month for your deposit? Add this to your budget planner. Is there now a shortfall? If so, how will you fill this? It could be an extra job or investing in yourself so that you get a promotion and a pay rise, or how about a side hustle?

Whatever the answer is, as long as it's legal and it balances the books, then go for it.

The Bank of Mum and Dad

Getting a handy bunk up the ladder is an amazing gift if you can get it. However, I often see people trying to stretch themselves too far to be able to help out their kids. So here are a few tips to help make sure a generous gift doesn't lead to a falling out!

- Don't just assume that you will get help. If you think you may get help or have heard it mentioned in passing, be brave and have the full conversation.

- If family members are willing to help, how much are they offering and what will the terms of the help be? Do they want you to pay it back? If so, when and how much?

- Will you be charged interest?

- Will you get it drawn up legally? This could be important if you are buying with a partner or friend and things go sour between you.

- What are the worst-case scenarios? What situations would lead to the money needing to be repaid and how would this be dealt with?

- Has inheritance tax advice been sought?
  This is especially important for large
  gifts.

Help from the Government

There are certain ISAs and government schemes available which are specifically designed to help first-time buyers.

Help to Buy ISA

Help to Buy ISAs were launched in 2015 to help people save to buy their first property. The government will give your cash savings a 25% boost. So for every £200 you save (the maximum that you can save each month), you get a government bonus of £50. The maximum total bonus you can get is £3,000. Therefore if you save £12,000, you will get an extra £3,000. There are a range of Help to Buy ISAs available from banks and building societies and the accounts are available per person and not per household – meaning you and your partner could both save. The government's bonus is paid in when you are ready to buy a property and your solicitor will need to apply for the bonus for you.

Do note, however, that there are restrictions on the value of the property you can buy. It mustn't be worth more than £250,000 if you are outside London or up to £450,000 if the property you are buying is in London.

Lifetime ISA

The Lifetime ISA (LISA) was launched in 2017 and although there aren't many providers offering this, it might be worthwhile looking into as a way to save for a house. The Lifetime ISA has similarities with the Help to Buy ISA in that it adds a 25% bonus for first-time buyers, but it also allows you to save a lot more. The differences are that the Lifetime ISA allows you to pay in lump sums, and bonuses are paid in annually so you can start to get interest or investment gains on the bonus too, rather than having to wait until you buy to claim it.

Here's what you need to know about LISAs:

- You can pay in up to £4,000 per annum.

- The government will add a 25% bonus annually (i.e. max £1,000 p. a.).

- It can be a savings account or an investment account.

- Remember that investments can go down as well as up.

- It is to help people buy their first home – as long as it costs £450,000 or less.

- Alternatively, or in addition, it can be used to save for retirement (after age sixty).

- You can open one at age eighteen.

- You can only open one if you are under forty.

- The bonus is paid every year until age fifty.

- If you take the money out for another reason you are penalized by 25%.

- You are not penalized if you die or are terminally ill.

- You can have a LISA as well as a Cash ISA/ Investment ISA.

- Couples can have one each even if you want to buy together.

- You can have a Help to Buy ISA and a LISA, but you can only use the bonus from one of them towards buying a home.

Lifetime ISAs have the additional benefit that if you are not using the money to buy your first property, you can also use the money for your retirement and still keep the bonus.

Help to Buy Equity Loan

This multi-billion-pound government scheme was introduced in 2013 and aims to help first-time buyers through offering them the opportunity to buy with only a 5% deposit and to borrow the rest of the deposit (up to 20% of the value of the home) from the government. The remaining 75% is then funded by a mortgage.

There are certain caveats to the scheme though: the home has to be a new-build house and the building company has to be taking part in the scheme. The government's loan is interest free for five years and it must be repaid either when the property is sold or the mortgage ends (after twenty-five years).

There is a slight difference for people who are buying in London as they can borrow up to 40% of the value of the house – twice the regular amount.

Shared Ownership

You can buy a share of your home (25–75%) and pay rent on the rest through a housing association. To qualify, your household income must be less than £80,000 per year or £90,000 per year in London. You must fit one of the following criteria:

- A first-time buyer.

- You used to own a home but cannot afford to buy one now.

- A current owner of a shared-ownership property.

Once you have bought your home through the scheme, you can then save up to purchase a bigger share – this is known as 'staircasing'. The cost of the new portion that you are buying will depend on the value of the property at the time you are buying the extra bit.

If you want to sell the property, the housing association has the right to buy it first, but if you own 100% of the property you are able to sell it freely.

Other House-buying Costs

Once you have your deposit, you will still need to consider the other costs associated with buying a property. Perhaps you will be able to use some of the money saved for your deposit to cover some of these costs, but will this strategy affect the price of what you can purchase? It's important to know about these costs and how you will save this money, so you need to add them on to your deposit goal total.

Stamp Duty

Stamp duty is a tax that you pay each time you buy a property as your main residence above £125,000. Politicians are constantly changing the rules depending on who they are trying to win votes from. The latest winners are first-time buyers who are buying in Northern Ireland or England. For properties up to £500,000, you will pay no stamp duty up to the first £300,000.

Stamp duty in Wales and Scotland is different, so be sure to check this out.

In Wales, Land Transaction Tax (LTT) has replaced stamp duty. It is charged in bands as follows:

Price Threshold	LTT Rate
Portion up to £180K	0%
Portion between £180K and £250K	3.5%
Portion between £250K and £400K	5%
Portion between £400K and £750K	7.5%
Portion between £750K and £1.5m	10%
Portion over £1.5m	12%

If you are buying a second property or a buy-to-let property in Wales rather than replacing your existing home then you will pay an extra 3% in stamp duty.

In Scotland it is called Land and Buildings Transaction Tax (LBTT). The rates increase in line with the purchase price of the property just like with stamp duty. You pay tax on the amounts between the bands rather than the full purchase price, just like you do with the Welsh LTT.

As with all of these things, when planning a property purchase (whether you're a first-time buyer or moving up the ladder) it is important to keep abreast of the rules so that you are not knocked off course. It is likely that any future changes will be announced in the Budget, which takes place in the autumn, and keep an eye out for the Spring Statement too in case there is anything in there. See the Resources section on p. 249 for more places to look. You might also find it useful to check out further advice on stamp duty on the www. gov.uk website.

Here are a few stamp duty examples:[1]

---

[1] Correct at June 2018.

Band	Normal Rate	Additional Property
Less than £145K	0%	3%
£145K–£250K	2%	5%
£250K–£325K	5%	8%
£325K–£750K	10%	13%
£750K +	12%	15%

Property Cost	First-time Buyer	Non First-time Buyer	Second Prop/ Buy to Let
£100,000	£0	£0	£3,000
£250,000	£0	£2,500	£10,000
£505,000	£15,250	£15,250	£30,400
£750,000	£27,500	£27,500	£50,000

Miscellaneous Costs

Unfortunately, buying a property costs more than the deposit and the stamp duty. Don't forget to budget for:

- **Valuation Fee:** Approx. £150–£1,500 depending on the property value. You might get a pleasant surprise though as some lenders don't always charge this.

- **Structural Survey:** £250–£600+.

- **Legal Fees:** £850–£1,500 plus VAT. Searches will also need to be paid for and these are approximately £250–£300.

- **Electronic Transfer Fee:** £40–£50 – this is for the lender to transfer the money to your solicitor.

- **Estate Agent's Fees:** It is best to get a quote but fees usually vary from 1–3% plus VAT.

- **Removal Costs:** £300–£600, though in my experience it can be much more than this depending on the service and how much stuff you are moving.

Doing Up Your Home

According to the Money Advice Service, it costs £5,750 in repairs for a new homeowner. Major works should be well thought through and budgeted into the plan before you put in an offer. Get quotes from two or three builders to get a broad guide. Make a 'Necessary' list for things that need doing immediately to make the place habitable, and another list for the work you'd like done but you can live without for a while. Your mortgage broker will be able to help you calculate what you can borrow in advance to cover immediate work. Funding for the 'we can live with it for a while' stuff can then be saved for and added into your budget planner.

It is important to have a contingency budget for any work carried out; most people say 10% is about right.

Finally, don't forget VAT! I have heard too many stories of people forgetting to add 20% VAT to their builders' quotes.

How to Nail the Right Mortgage Rate

Unless you are really lucky, it is likely that you are going to need the help of a mortgage to work your way up the property ladder. Here are a few rules of thumb when it comes to mortgages to help you work out how you are going to do it and what you'll need to save.

The maximum you can borrow is often four or five times your earnings. If you are buying with someone else you may be able to borrow four or five times joint earnings.

The amount of deposit you put down will impact how good a mortgage rate you can get. The general cut-offs are 5%, 10%, 15% and 25%, with the very best rates available for those with 40% deposits. If you have a 13% deposit, for example, you might find you are better off waiting that little bit longer to save that little bit more. A good independent mortgage broker will help you to work through the maths, or else there are loads of great online mortgage calculators you can use to help you work out what you need to put aside to achieve your goal.

Using a Mortgage Broker

I encourage all of my clients to use the services of an independent mortgage broker for the following reasons:

- They will be able to search the whole market to get you the very best mortgage for your situation.

- They will take your full financial situation and future plans into account when suggesting a product and term.

- If your situation is not straightforward, they will be able to speak directly to a range of lenders before applying to make sure that when you do apply you actually get accepted. This will avoid you getting any black marks on your credit report which may spook future lenders.

- They do all the hard work for you!

In my view, they are always worth it. Most importantly, make sure they are independent rather than only able to sell certain lenders' mortgages. Find someone you like and who you know will have your best interests at heart. Asking friends and family for recommendations is probably the best place to start. Alternatively, you can check the Resources section on p. 250 for tips on how to find a broker.

A final word of warning: not all mortgage brokers are equal! Make sure you are aware that different lenders will pay brokers different levels of commission for a mortgage of the same value. Less conscientious ones may be swayed by the higher commission rather than your best interests.

Mortgage Term Decisions

When arranging your mortgage, you have many decisions to make and the biggest one is the term, i.e. how long it will take to pay off the mortgage completely. The longer the term, the less you will pay each month, but the more interest you will pay back over time.

The table opposite shows you the total cost of borrowing £100,000 at various interest rates and different terms. As you can see, a longer term doesn't add a huge amount at low interest rates to the amount you pay over all. For example, if you had a mortgage at 2% interest over twenty years, you would pay back only £11,661 less than if you had a thirty-year term. However, if interest rates were to really increase and you found yourself with a whopping 7% rate of interest, you would end up paying

Examples of Costs Over Term and Total Interest Paid Per £100,000

	20 Years	25 Years	30 Years
2%	(£506pm) & £121,429	(£424pm) & £127,179	(£370pm) & £133,090
3%	(£555pm) & £133,085	(£474pm) & £142,239	(£422pm) & £151,747
5%	(£660pm) & £158,437	(£585pm) & £175,441	(£537pm) & £193,338
7%	(£775pm) & £186,086	(£707pm) & £212,051	(£665pm) & £239,536

an extra £56,450 on a thirty-year term compared to a twenty-year term.

As you can see, per £100,000 there is not a huge difference in monthly repayment costs – if you wanted to be committed to becoming mortgage free as quickly as possible, a little extra goes a long way. We are in an artificially low period of interest rates at the moment and it is very easy to think of this as the norm. Interest rates drastically alter the amount you pay back over the period. Over thirty years you can see that at 2% you pay back almost a third of the interest you would at 5%! Now is a great time to get a mortgage plan of action whilst interest rates are so low.

It might sound obvious but so many people forget to make sure that their actual mortgage end date is aligned to their ideal mortgage end date. Just because you can now get mortgages way past sixty-five, it doesn't mean you have to. Having your mortgage fixed to your ideal retirement age also means you don't have to use any of your pension to pay it off.

Overpaying a mortgage

Overpaying a mortgage plays a key part in meeting long-term financial goals. By overpaying your mortgage you are able to build up equity in your property (if markets on average rise), which will help you to buy a bigger place in the future and move up the ladder. It is also a crucial planning tool if you know in the future your outgoings or income are likely to change in a way that puts you under pressure, e.g. if your outgoings increase (with, say, school or university fees), or if your income decreases (you decide to take a sabbatical).

The Buying Process

1) Speak to a mortgage broker to work out the maximum you can borrow. Don't get carried away! This really is the maximum – your dream home will always be that extra few thousand/ tens of thousands/hundreds of thousands away. You can estimate your affordability and monthly payments at different purchase/deposit ratios by using online mortgage calculators.

2) Think about costs and worst-case scenarios. You may be able to afford the new house, but can you afford to turn the lights on and the season ticket to work? Lots of property websites can now provide estimates of what the running costs will be. Do a full budget planner like the one we did at the beginning of the book, imagining all your outgoings in the new house.

3) Work out what's important to you. What will you compromise on and what will you not? But be flexible. Every property I have bought has always been at the edge of my predetermined

comfort zone. When buying my first flat I was set on a garden, but I ended up ditching the garden idea in order to have a bigger place two minutes' walk from the station. What about schools? This may not be on your radar now but it might well be before you sell the property. A good school in the area is also a great reason for someone to buy the property from you in the future.

4) Sell yourself to the estate agent. I always find it helps to be proactive when dealing with agents and letting them know you are a serious buyer. They will meet lots of buyers (especially in boom times) so it is important that you stick out in their mind as someone reliable, who turns up to appointments on time and has a clear idea of what they want and can afford. Importantly too, though, don't let the estate agents lead you astray. Be clear about what you are trying to achieve and in which areas.

5) Once you have found a property you would like to buy it is time to put your offer in, usually via an estate agent. You can put the offer in verbally but I think it is sensible to follow this up with an email too. The agent is then obliged to pass this offer on to the vendor. When putting in the offer it can help if you remind the estate agent about why you are a good

buyer – don't assume that vendors always choose on price alone. Important things to mention are if you are chain free and how quickly you want to move. Whether your offer is accepted or not, the estate agent must send confirmation of the offer to you in writing.

If your initial offer is not accepted, don't panic. If you can afford to, perhaps you can offer more, or maybe your offer will become more appealing if the offer that was accepted doesn't work out. A note of warning though – don't get swept up in an offer frenzy! If you can't afford the property at the new price, it obviously was not meant to be.

If your offer is accepted, make sure the estate agent has taken the property off the market and that it's no longer advertising the property to new prospective buyers. Now it's time to move fast!

6) Get your mortgage broker back on the case. The mortgage broker will complete the lender's application form and let you have a list of all the documents they need. If you aren't using a mortgage broker you need to do the application for yourself (the lender will send the application forms to you) and in some cases they can do them over the phone with you. Make sure you

do not make any errors on the forms as this can delay the mortgage approval.

7) Choose a solicitor – the solicitor will be in charge of the conveyancing, the process that enables a property to change ownership. The first port of call is to see if your mortgage deal comes with free legals and, if so, there will be a panel of solicitors that you can choose from.

If you need to find your own solicitor, ask for recommendations from family and friends and perhaps the estate agent too. Make sure you are choosing someone who is a member of the Law Society and also a member of the Law Society's Conveyancing Quality scheme. Be mindful, there could be a conflict of interest if you use the solicitor connected to the estate agent because they would know what the maximum is that you are able to buy for.

8) Valuation – the mortgage lender will now want to carry out a valuation on the property. This will give the lender an idea of whether your offer was too high or if it was fair. Keep on top of this to ensure it is completed and keep the estate agent informed.

9) Surveys – you may want to consider getting a comprehensive survey done on the property, especially if you are buying an older property.

These are called Homebuyer Surveys and they can avoid unforeseen repair costs down the line. Worryingly, according to the Royal Institute of Chartered Surveyors, only one in five people get this survey done.

If your survey reveals problems with the property, don't be afraid to speak up. If you pull out, other buyers are only going to find the same thing (assuming they get a survey done). Firstly, check if any of the problems are covered by a guarantee. Then ask the surveyor what they think it will cost to solve the problem and for major works also speak to a few builders. These estimates can then be used to renegotiate your offer to take them into account. It is important to remember that the cost of the repair work may not only be financial. You could end up living in a building site for months! So ask if the vendors could complete the work before you move in.

10) Keep the momentum going, keeping all lines of communications open, especially if things aren't going to plan.

11) Exchange – this is the last point at which you can still pull out. Make sure you are certain. Make sure all the queries have been answered, then you can go ahead and sign the contract with the legal advice of your solicitor. Once

Buy to Let: An Investment or Not?

This section could be a book on its own, but I have kept it short because I don't want an investment property to detract from you doing the basics well. It's always a worry when new clients come to see me and their answer to all their financial planning questions is 'my buy-to-let is my pension' or 'we'd just sell the buy-to-let'. This is not exact financial planning and, as we are seeing now, the buy-to-let streets aren't always paved with gold! A second property needs to be well thought through once you have got your savings, pension, investments and insurance boxes ticked – and not before.

I bought a buy-to-let property in 2016 when my kids were babies as a way to invest for their future. In the short time that we have owned the property we could have made more money by investing in funds as the property hasn't gone up in value.

Investing in a property comes with different rules and here are some important things to know:

- You need a bigger deposit – 25% used to be ideal but this has changed over the last few years and, in order to make an investment viable, it is not uncommon to need deposits of 30–40%.

- You pay income tax on the rental income and capital gains tax on any profits you make from the property going up in value.

- Most people have interest-only mortgages on buy-to-lets; however, what's the end game? How will you pay the mortgage off if you need the income for retirement, will you sell the property? What's the right mortgage for you?

- Don't forget that you will incur an extra 3% in stamp duty on any buy-to-let purchase.

- You will need a contingency fund saved up to take care of any void periods – even if no one is living in your property paying you rent, you will still owe the mortgage provider.

- Don't forget to find out if there is a service charge on the property and, if so, what it is and when it's payable.

- When you buy, don't forget to consider if it will be easy to sell. A new build will not look so shiny and new a few decades down the line.

you have exchanged, you will need buildings
insurance in place to cover the property.

12) Completion – this is money time! You now
need to transfer the money that you owe to
your solicitor's account. Make sure you are
transferring the money to a legitimate account
as this has been a ripe ground for fraudsters
in the past. You will also need to pay the
mortgage account fee (if applicable) plus
your solicitor's bill, and once this is done the
solicitor can register the sale with the land
registry. Finally, you need to pay your stamp
duty – as we have seen, this will vary
depending on the cost of your property.

Mortgage Jargon Buster

Agreement in Principle (AIP): A letter from a mortgage lender confirming the amount that they will be willing to lend. This is proof to the vendor of the property you are hoping to buy that you can afford the property. This can also be known as a Mortgage in Principle (MIP).

Annual Percentage Rate (APR): The total cost of a mortgage including interest and fees. It is often used to compare deals between providers.

Arrangement Fee: A fee that is charged to set up a mortgage. Remember that if you add this to the loan then you will pay interest on this too.

Bank of England Base Rate: The Bank of England's Monetary Policy Committee meet regularly and they are responsible for controlling inflation. Currently, they have a target to keep inflation at 2% and they use interest rates to control inflation. Tracker and standard variable rate mortgages usually follow the Bank of England rate.

Buildings Insurance: This insurance covers you should your home be damaged, e.g. through flooding/fire. It is usually a requirement of your mortgage to have this in place.

Buy to Let: A property that is bought to let out to tenants. Mortgage lenders offer different mortgage deals to buy-to-let investors than for a residential property. Usually you need a larger deposit and the interest rates are higher.

Capped and Collared Rates: A type of mortgage deal that is linked to the Bank of England base rate but which has an upper limit that it will not exceed even if the base rate rises. A mortgage can also have a collar which means that the interest rate you pay will not fall below a certain rate.

Conveyancing: The legal process of buying a property, usually done by a solicitor.

County Court Judgement (CCJ): A County Court Judgement is made against you if you don't meet the payments to maintain your debts. If you have a CCJ it will make getting a mortgage much more difficult.

Deposit: The amount of cash you put down when you are buying a property. The best mortgage rates are usually reserved for people with the biggest deposit. The rest of the property is then bought with a mortgage.

Discounted Rate Mortgages: A mortgage with an interest rate that is linked to the lender's standard variable rate (SVR). The rate will be discounted in relation to the SVR, e.g. 1% below SVR.

Early Repayment Charges/Penalties: These have to be paid if you leave your mortgage, e.g. move to a new lender or pay off your mortgage (above agreed amounts), during a specified period.

Endowment Mortgage: A mortgage which is interest only (i.e. you never pay the amount you owe back), but instead pay (usually monthly) into an investment called an endowment. The theory is that the investment grows at a higher rate than your interest is costing you and at the end of the mortgage term you use the investment to pay off the whole mortgage. Endowments usually have life cover for your mortgage included too. However, the reality is that endowments have not performed as well as people hoped and as a consequence have become less popular in the last decade or so.

Equity: The amount of a property that you own (i.e. is not covered by a mortgage). This is usually your deposit plus anything that you have paid off over time, along with any growth in house prices.

Equity Release: This allows a homeowner (usually an older person who is retired) to release some of the equity in their property so they can spend it now rather than having to sell the property or simply pass on the property on their death.

Family Offset Mortgages: These are a relatively new idea and are usually used by parents/family members who wish to help a first-time buyer on to the property ladder. The savings of the family member are offset against the amount of the mortgage so that the first-time buyer has a bigger deposit and thus reduces the amount of mortgage needed and therefore interest paid. This is especially appealing whilst interest rates on savings are very low.

Fixed Rate Mortgage: A mortgage where the rate of interest is fixed for a set period of time. The benefit of this is that if interest rates rise, your mortgage will not be affected and it therefore offers some security that you know what you will be paying. For example, if you are on a five-year fixed rate at 3% you know that for the next five years your mortgage payments will remain at 3%.

Flexible Mortgage: These mortgages allow you to overpay, underpay and take breaks from paying your mortgage. The downside of these mortgages is that you tend to have to pay a higher interest rate than you would if your mortgage was not flexible.

Freehold: This means you own the land that your property is built on. You can also own a share of freehold if, for example, a house has been split into two flats.

Gazumping: This is when you have had an offer accepted on a property and then your offer gets trumped by another buyer with a higher offer, which is then accepted by the seller.

Guarantor: Someone (a third party) who agrees to meet your mortgage payments if you are unable to. A guarantor is a particularly common requirement for first-time buyers.

Help to Buy: Government schemes that aim to make house buying more affordable and therefore easier.

Help to Buy ISA: A tax-free savings account the government will reward you for saving into. The government will pay you 25% of everything you save, up to a maximum of £3,000 per annum. So if you pay in £200, they will pay in £50.

Interest Only Mortgage: A type of mortgage where you only pay off the interest that you owe rather than a proportion of the capital (the amount you borrowed). The aim is that you save enough money personally to pay off the mortgage at the end. Sometimes people use the lump sum from their pension to pay off a smaller mortgage. If you fail to save the money, at the end of the mortgage term you will not own your entire home and will have to sell and either downsize or rent.

Joint Tenants: When you buy a house with another person and you have 'equal rights to the whole property'. The

property automatically goes to the other person if one of
you dies.

Key Worker Schemes: A key worker is a public sector
worker who is considered to provide an essential service,
e.g. nurses and police. The government forces developers
to allocate a certain percentage of properties to key
workers at affordable prices.

Land Registry: The official body that keeps track of who
owns which property.

Leasehold: This means that you own the building but not the
land that it is built on. These properties will have a lease for
a certain period of time (e.g. 999 years) and usually you can
choose to pay to extend the lease if you have a short lease.
If your lease is short (say sixty to seventy years), you may
find it difficult to get a mortgage and also to sell the
property.

Loan to Value (LTV): This is your mortgage as a percentage
of the property value. For example, if I have a £50,000
mortgage on a £500,000 property my LTV is 10%.

Mortgage Term: The length of time you will have a mortgage
for, e.g. twenty-five years. This is not to be confused with
the mortgage deal term as this could be, say, two, three or
five years before you need to look around to see if you can
get a better deal. At the end of your mortgage term, on a
capital repayment mortgage, you will own the property in full.

Negative Equity: This is when the amount you owe on the
mortgage is more than the value of the property, i.e. you
owe £200,000 and the value is only £150,000.

Offset Mortgage: This is where your savings accounts are linked to your mortgage. If, for example, you owe £150,000 on your mortgage but you have an emergency cash savings fund of £20,000, you will only pay interest on the difference, i.e. £130,000. You do have easy access to your savings though and so you can withdraw them at any time. This is especially appealing when savings rates are lower than the interest rate that you are paying on your mortgage.

Portable Mortgage: If a mortgage is portable, it means you can take the mortgage with you if you move house. The benefit of this is that you won't suffer Early Repayment Penalties (ERP) if you move house whilst you are still tied in to your mortgage deal.

Remortgaging: This is when you change your mortgage at the end of your mortgage deal. It doesn't mean you have to move house.

Repayment Mortgage: A type of mortgage where each month you pay the interest and some of the capital (the amount you owe). As long as you don't miss any payments, this guarantees that you will own your home outright at the end of the term.

Right to Buy: This was initially a scheme to enable council tenants to buy the homes they rented and it's now open to some housing association tenants too.

Service Charge: A fee that is payment to a managing agent to maintain a leasehold property. It typically pays for upkeep of communal areas, lifts and gardens, etc.

Shared Ownership: You own a percentage of a property rather than the whole amount. The rest is typically owned by a housing association. You pay rent on the portion the housing association own. Over time you can ask to purchase a bigger share of a property.

Stamp Duty Land Tax (SDLT): A tax payable each time you buy a property.

Standard Variable Rate (SVR): The default interest rate of the mortgage lender. If you do not remortgage at the end of your deal, you will switch on to your lender's SVR. This could mean a huge hike in the amount of interest you are paying.

Subprime Mortgage: A mortgage for people with bad credit problems.

Tenants in Common: This is when you own a property with another person but you have chosen to buy a certain share each. On death the share of the property is not automatically passed on to the other shareholder(s). See Joint Tenants to learn more.

Tracker Mortgage: A mortgage that tracks the Bank of England's base rate. So if it goes up, your mortgage interest will go up, which means that your monthly payments will go up. The reverse happens if the Bank of England's base rate goes down.

Valuation Survey: Lenders always carry out a valuation survey to check if the house is worth what you are buying it for. A survey can also look at the structure of the property to see if there are any problems with the building.

Variable Rate Mortgage: A mortgage that can go down or up with your lender's standard variable rate.

Yield: The return you get on a property when considering the rental expressed as a percentage of the capital that you have invested.

5
WHAT COMES NEXT?

As we get older, our priorities in life change – we often want more of those things that come with much bigger price tags! So how do we plan to be sure we can find all this extra money without straying from our budgets? In this chapter we will tackle planning for some of those big life events at different milestones.

How Much is that Doggy in the Window?

For some people, pets are like a child and they can certainly feel like they cost the same at times!

According to Sainsbury's, the lifetime cost of owning a dog is almost £17,000 and this figure is slightly more for a cat. The annual cost of owning a dog is £1,183. Add up the expected costs for your desired pet and put them into your budget planner to give you an idea of whether you can really afford it.

Things like jabs, insurance and food pale into insignificance when you think about the cost of a dog walker, let alone the cost of kennels or pet-sitting when you go on holiday, so here are my top tips for saving money as a pet owner:

- Adopt rather than buy – there are so many animals that need a good home. They might not be the designer dog you had in mind, but it doesn't mean you will love them any less once you welcome them into your home.

- Buy pet food in bulk – you can get huge savings by having it delivered in bulk rather than adding it to your weekly food shop.

- Consider a pet-sitting exchange with a friend to save on costs when you go on holiday.

- When buying pet insurance, get the balance right between your excess and your monthly payments – generally the higher the excess the lower the monthly payment. Just be sure you are able to pay the excess if you need to.

- Some insurers will offer you a discount if you have multiple animals insured with them.

- Check how much you can save if you pay your pet insurance annually rather than monthly.

- Sign up for loyalty programmes with your pet food supplier or local pet shop.

- Have a look at websites where pet lovers sign up to play with/walk your dog for free as an alternative to paying for this service. Would you feel happy to do this?

Walking Down the Aisle – For Richer, For Poorer

The cost of a wedding can be HUGE! I have helped numerous clients fork out six-figure sums to fund their child's wedding, and according to *Brides* magazine, the average UK wedding cost is £24,000. This is a fortune and, like anything to do with money, it is important to first consider what you are trying to achieve and what will make the day special for you. Whatever the budget, there are always going to be compromises to make. For me and my husband, we decided that the most import-ant thing for us was that people had a huge amount of fun and that there was a party atmosphere. To provide a free bar, we compromised on food and ditched the posh canapés.

Fill in the table below to figure out what's important for your big day.

What are my top five priorities?

What are the five things that aren't important to me?

What have been the things I have liked most at other people's weddings?

What have I not liked at other people's weddings?

What traditions are not important/ are important to me?

Don't forget that this is usually a joint decision, so perhaps your partner-to-be should fill out a version of this plan too, to make sure you prioritize the things that are important to you both.

Planning and Budgeting for a Wedding

The first thing to work out is what you can afford to spend on a wedding. How does this expenditure impact other financial goals? Would you rather have a smaller wedding and a bigger house deposit for example?

Will your parents help out? Have THE chat! If so, how much and – as when we discussed the bank of mum and dad in the last chapter – are there any criteria that come with the gift?

Once you know what you have to spend and know how long you have to save, fill out the wedding budget planner on p. 145 and allocate a number to each expenditure using your best guess. This will help you to keep track of what you are over/underspending on and you can work out easily what to cut back on if you are overspending on a particular area that is important to you. Don't forget to add an emergency buffer to take care of any last-minute emergencies that may crop up.

My top wedding plan budgeting tips

- When you are saving money for your wedding, put it away in a separate account so it can't get

MARC AND MARIE'S WEDDING BUDGET – JULY 2018

MARC AND MARIE TOTAL MONEY COMING IN		£30,000.00
PAY-INS	From Aunty	£1,000.00
	From Grandma	£1,000.00
	From Mum and Dad	£7,500.00
SUB TOTAL		£9,500.00
THE BIG SPENDS	Venue	£6,000.00
	Food	£8,000.00
	Drink	£3,000.00
	Wedding Dress	£2,000.00
	Groom's Outfit	£500.00
	Bridesmaids' Outfits	£800.00
	Ushers' Outfits	£800.00
	Flowers	£1,500.00
	Photography	£2,500.00
	Accommodation	£800.00
	Hair and Make-up	£600.00
	Honeymoon	£5,000.00
	Transport	£700.00
	Rings	£1,500.00
	Cake	£750.00
	Band	£2,500.00
SUB TOTAL		£36,950.00
THE FINISHING TOUCHES	Stationery	£200.00
	Wedding Favours	£500.00
	Presents for Parents	£200.00
	Presents for Wedding Party	£300.00
	Bride's Shoes	£300.00
	Bride's Jewellery	£200.00
	Table Decorations	£100.00
	Church (Choir, Bells etc.)	£300.00
	Bunting	£100.00
	Welcome Signs	£50.00
	Candles	£50.00
SUB TOTAL		£2,300.00
LEFT		£250.00

Budget/Estimate	Deposit Paid	Final Date Paid	By Whom

accidentally mixed in with your day-to-day spending.

- Make sure you pick a wedding date that you know you can manage to have all your finances in place for.

- Have a contingency/secret slack in your budget where possible.

- Don't forget why you are doing this and what's important – before bridezilla sets in!

- Be prepared to rethink your ideas and potentially ditch or downgrade some elements.

- Shop around for the best deals and don't be scared to negotiate or ask for cheaper alternatives.

- Speak to married friends regarding what they spent to get a real feel for what things cost in your area.

- Be ready to accept help from family and friends who are talented in certain areas. Perhaps they could offer their services instead of a wedding present?

- Watch the small spends as these can really add up, e.g. candles, favours, place settings, etc.

- Opt for flowers that have a large head to reduce the number of blooms you need.

- Don't forget the costs related to registering your marriage – currently £46.

- Don't over-cater – a fifth of all wedding food is thrown away!

- A simple way to keep the cost down is to only invite people who are genuinely close to you and that you like. Keep the guest list down to those who are important to you.

- Research the different prices at different times of year – if you're basing your decision on weather, don't forget it can still rain in the more costly August!

DINKY – Double Income No Kids Yet

This really is, with hindsight, the time of your life. DINKY is a phase of your life when you are settling down as a couple but don't have the financial commitments of kids. A lot of my clients remain in the DINKY phase for their whole life and as a consequence are able to amass huge amounts of wealth that is often used to retire early/ travel extensively/buy that amazing second property.

For others, DINKY is that time when you move in together, don't have kids and are usually both working. Your disposable income is high and as a percentage could well be higher than it will be for a long time into the future.

If you are in the DINKY phase, revisit your goals and see if you can adjust your budget to make the most of this high level of disposable income.

Doing it for the Kids

How much does having a baby really cost? Answer: a fortune! The 'Cost of a Child' report from 2017 shows that to raise a child (excluding housing, council tax and childcare) costs £75,436 for a couple and £102,627 for a lone parent. The insurer Liverpool Victoria (LV) has calculated that the total cost of raising a child to twenty-one is over £250,000. This is for state school education; if you add in private school it jumps to £373,000, and to £500,000 for boarding school.

When is the Right Time Financially?

There is so much to think about once you have made the decision that you would like to have a family. Money can play a key role. Is where you are living now big enough? Would you need to move if you had a second child? Who will look after the child? Will you go back to work? Will you split maternity and paternity care? A few years down the line and the financial thoughts turn more towards education and catchment areas, after-school clubs, paying for uniform, holidays at peak times, etc. . . .

Where the money goes (LV 2016)

Childcare and babysitting	£70,466
Education-linked expenses (trips/uniform/school lunch, etc.)	£74,430
Clothing	£10,942
Other	£14,195
Holidays	£16,882
Food	£19,004
Furniture	£3,408
Pocket money	£4,614
Personal	£1,130
Leisure and recreation	£7,464
Hobbies and toys	£9,307

There might never be a 'perfect time' financially to start a family. Money was my biggest worry when we were thinking about having children and fretting about money consumed a lot of my thoughts when I was pregnant. My husband and I also gave ourselves the biggest headaches work-wise too. I had just moved my advisory business to a new firm and my husband had just gone self-employed, so we felt very unsettled financially. There were a million reasons to just 'wait an extra year' but in the end we bit the bullet.

The first year costs the most and it is not surprising really when you consider all the items that are marketed to you as an 'essential' buy. It feels like there is a gadget for everything! It costs on average £11,498 to have a child in their first year.

When I was pregnant with our first child, we used a baby list with a department store, which is like a wedding list but for when you have a child. This meant that family who wanted to help out could buy from the list, but it was also really helpful to get advice from the staff about what was essential and what was not. I was so glad to have all the breastfeeding accessories (nipple shields, etc.) that I wouldn't have thought to buy myself. At the same time, it was helpful to see the total cost of everything in one go. That way we were able to cut the list to suit our budget before pressing 'go'.

Maternity/Paternity Leave

Couples can now share time off work for the first year of their child's life. Mums can take fifty-two weeks off and share up to fifty weeks with their partner. The first two weeks are mandatory. Each parent will be paid by their employer for their portion of the time off. The going rate is currently the lower of either £139.58 per week or 90% of your average weekly salary for a maximum of thirty-nine weeks.

Your employer may choose to pay you extra, so it is worthwhile looking into their maternity policy as far ahead as possible. It's even more important to do this if you are planning a family and a career move within a short space of time.

Maternity/Paternity if Self-employed

The benefit that self-employed mothers are entitled to is called Maternity Allowance, but only if they have paid Class 2 National Insurance for at least thirteen weeks of the sixty-six weeks before their baby is due. To claim, you need to download the form from the government's website and then send it in for assessment. As a general rule of thumb, the maximum you can get is £145.18 per week.

There is no cover for self-employed dads at the moment, sadly, and this is definitely something that should be changed. It really seems unfair and feels like a double standard for the government to enforce companies to offer shared parental leave but to not standardize their benefits for the self-employed.

Child Benefit

You can claim Child Benefit if you are responsible for looking after a child who is under sixteen or until twenty if they are in full-time education, and there is no limit to how many children you can claim for. Until recently anyone could get this benefit but now it has become means tested to make sure you are not claiming when you shouldn't be.

You will get full child benefit if you (and your partner) earn less than £50,000 each.

Child benefit pays out at £20.70 per week for the eldest child and then £13.70 for any additional children.

If your income is over £50,000 then you may have to pay a tax charge which will reduce the amount you are entitled to, and if you earn over £60,000 then you are not entitled to claim any Child Benefit.

The earnings cap applies if either partner earns over £60,000 individually. It is nothing to do with total household income, so if you are both earning £49,999 then you can still claim the maximum benefit. If one earns £65,000 and the other nothing, then you are not eligible to claim.

Childcare Options

The UK is one of the most expensive places on the planet when it comes to childcare. It is not uncommon to be paying £40–£60 per day and in London prices can be anything up to £90–£100 per day.

The government runs two childcare schemes that you need to know about.

Childcare vouchers

Childcare vouchers are offered by many workplaces as part of their benefits package. You can buy the vouchers via salary sacrifice (i.e. before tax and National Insurance). Basic rate tax payers can claim £243 per month per parent and higher rate tax payers can claim £625 per month whilst additional rate tax payers can claim £623 per month.

Tax-free childcare

This scheme came into force in April 2017. It will eventually replace childcare vouchers but for now the two schemes are running concurrently. The state will pay £20 for every £80 you spend on childcare (i.e. basic rate tax relief). The maximum contribution you can get from the government is £2,000 per annum. You are eligible if you work more than sixteen hours per week and earn less than £100,000. You can have a joint income of more than £100,000, as the limit is per person. So if as a couple you both earn £99,999 then you will both qualify. But if one parent works, you will only qualify for fifteen hours of childcare per week.

You apply by opening a childcare account that you pay into and the government will top it up for you. (You can do this via www.gov.uk/get-tax-free-childcare.)

Don't forget this is not just there for preschooling. You can use the money for after-school and holiday clubs too as long as the providers are registered.

Unfortunately you cannot apply for both of these schemes and you now have to choose between the two options. Here is an easy-to-read breakdown that will help you in your decision-making.

As a general rule of thumb, tax-free childcare is best for those with more than one child as the savings are per child, and childcare vouchers are best if you earn over £100,000.

Thirty hours 'free'

Children who are three and four are now entitled to thirty hours' free early education childcare. This has recently increased from fifteen hours per week. The hours must be spread over three or more days for at least thirty-eight weeks of the year. To qualify, you must work more than sixteen hours a week and earn less than £100,000.

You should be able to access the funding through some childminders, preschools and out-of-school providers. However, before getting your hopes up you should do your research. A lot of places aren't offering the thirty hours because the rate they get reimbursed at doesn't cover the

Tax-free childcare	Childcare vouchers
Up to when the child is twelve	Up to when the child is fifteen
No National Insurance saving	National Insurance saving via salary sacrifice
£100,000 earnings limit to qualify	No earnings limit
Open to all qualifying people	Only available if offered by employer
Open to self-employed	Not available to self-employed

cost of providing the care – especially in more expensive areas of the country.

Working Tax Credit

There is an element of the Working Tax Credit that is to help with childcare cost. According to Moneysaving expert.com the average childcare element of the Working Tax Credit is £60 per week – £3,120 per annum – definitely not to be sniffed at! So do you qualify?

- Are you a single parent working sixteen-plus hours a week or in a couple both working sixteen-plus hours a week?

- Is your total household income under £46,000?

If the answer to both of the above is 'yes', then you should be eligible for Working Tax Credit.

Retirement and Long-term Planning

Many of my clients love their jobs or running their own business and hate the idea of being retired. However, going to work on a dark Monday morning is a very different experience if you are getting out of bed because you want to, rather than because you have to. So instead of asking the question, 'When do you want to retire?' I ask, 'When do you want to have enough money so that you are going to work because you want to rather than you have to?'

People tend to fall into two camps: those who want to be financially secure in their fifties (or earlier) – perhaps because this is what their parents did – and those who say, 'Dunno – aren't I going to have to work until my seventies?'

In my view, both responses have missed the mark.

Firstly, this is your retirement, it's time to enjoy a well-deserved rest after years of hard work, so your answer needs to be more thoroughly thought through. For example: 'Well, travel is very important to me so I would like to ensure that I have at least five holidays a year costing £X once the kids have grown up (when I am in my fifties) until my early eighties. I would like to downsize and have a home in Manchester and one in Spain so that I can live between the two the rest of the time. My standard of living in today's prices will cost £X per annum.'

This response tells me far more about what will make the client happy financially and about what is important to them. Now when planning this client's retirement, I know what income they need and I will put in place a plan that will ensure they have enough money to stop work altogether at fifty-seven. If they choose to continue to work full- or part-time, it just means there will be more money in the pot.

As you will have noticed by now, there is a theme running through this book: those who have a plan and know what they want tend to get closer to achieving their goals.

Have a think about what you want to do in retirement. What's important to you? Don't forget, too, that when you are in your sixties, you will not be the same person that you are today. A week of misbehaving in Mykonos probably won't be at the top of your agenda any more. Perhaps you will be motivated by holidays, writing that book you have always promised yourself, charitable work, or maybe even having the money behind you to start your second career.

So, do the best you can at answering these questions:

- When do I want to retire? Will it be a fixed day when all of a sudden I don't work any more or will I have more of a phased retirement?

- How will I spend my time?

- Where will I spend my time and with whom?

- What will make me feel happy and fulfilled?

Secondly, retirement is not only about what you do at sixty, it is also about how you see out your last years on the planet. Old age can be very isolating and very stressful, especially when you are surviving off the state pension alone. Personally, I would like to have enough money to stay in my home as long as possible, opting to bring people in to care for me, and I would like enough money to afford to get out (taxis) and to busy myself (clubs/lunches, etc.). All of which will help me to maintain a positive outlook on life so that I can enjoy myself. Are there any retired relatives/neighbours/friends who you can chat with to help you work out what's important to you?

How Much Do You Need to Retire?

How long is a piece of string? It all depends on what you would like to spend and the standard of living you have in mind. Take a look at your budget planner and adapt it for retirement. You may not be paying off a mortgage or debt (hopefully), but you will have more free time to spend money and you are likely to take more holidays in your early retirement.

A good place to start working out what lump sum you are aiming for is the 4% rule. For every £4,000 of annual income you want, you need at least £100,000. So if you need £20,000, you need a whopping £500,000! This doesn't all have to be in pensions, but in cash (not too much), investments and perhaps equity in a buy-to-let.

Now, given that the average pension pot for a man is around £75,000 and for a woman is £25,000, is it any wonder there are so many people feeling the pinch in retirement?

Pensions

Pensions often get a bad press. People tend to not like them but don't really know why, and the media exacerbate this problem by only reporting the negative headlines. What you need to know is that a pension is an investment account that gives you tax benefits for delayed gratification, i.e. you are not allowed to spend the money until you are at least fifty-five, so to reward you for putting money aside for the future, the government gives you tax relief.

The main problem with pensions is that people really underestimate how much you need to put into them. If you work from the ages of twenty to sixty and then live until you are a hundred, you will have been retired for as long as you had been working. If you want to maintain the same standard of living you had when working, you are going to need to stash away a decent amount, and you are going to need to keep on top of it, because what you get at the end will depend on what you put away, and how well your investments perform.

It is imperative that you don't file retirement planning into the 'to do later' pile. The following sections will help you to understand the types of pensions, how they work and also what you should be doing.

Why Pay into a Pension?

The best benefit of a pension (and one often disregarded by critics) is that pensions are super tax efficient. If you pay in, the government pays in. Here's how it works if you pay in £100:

- **Basic rate tax payers:** The government pays in £25, so your total payment is £125.

- **Higher rate tax payers:** The government pays in £66.67, so your total payment is £166.67.

- **Additional rate tax payers:** The government pays in £81.81, so your total payment is £181.81.

As you can see, you are effectively getting a refund of the tax you have paid to earn the £100 in the first place. If you are paying your pension through a work scheme, you may be able to pay in via salary sacrifice. This means the money goes into your pension before tax is deducted, so not only do you save National Insurance but you don't have to do a tax return to claim back the money.

If you are paying into a personal pension then you do need to do a tax return if you are a higher or additional rate tax payer. This is because the government applies tax relief automatically with your pension company as if you were a basic rate tax payer; the other tax payers have to claim it back via their tax return. If you are panicking because you haven't done this before and even believe you are owed tax relief, you are allowed to claim back four years. Act quickly before you miss out.

You can pay in up to 100% of your earnings or £40,000 (including the tax relief), whichever is the highest, and still get tax relief. This is called the annual allowance. There are exemptions though for those earning upwards of £150,000 and exceptionally high earners can only pay in £10,000.

You can access your pension at fifty-five (although this age is set to increase to fifty-seven) and you can still work and access your pension at the same time.

When you take your pension, 25% is tax free and this is known as the Pension Commencement Lump Sum (PCLS). The rest of the income that you take is taxed as if it was a salary. In theory you could take all the money out of your pension on your fifty-fifth birthday, but this may result in a huge unwanted tax bill!

Finally, if you do too well at your retirement planning, the maximum you can accumulate into your pension is £1,000,000. If you go over this there will be tax consequences.

Since 2004, pensions have become far more user friendly and flexible. So if you are naturally negative about pensions – and this could be something you have inherited from your parents – perhaps it is time to revisit the issue and see if you should reconsider.

How Much Should You be Paying into Your Pension?

As a general rule of thumb, the total (including your employer's contribution) should be half your age as a percentage of your income. For example, if I am thirty I should be paying 15% of my income into a pension. Now, before you panic, this is a target, not a starting place! It is far more important to actually get started and to build on it rather than waiting until you earn more because you feel you will be able to afford it. The reason is that you will never feel that you can afford it. When you think about it, most people work from the age of twenty until they are sixty (forty years) and could reasonably expect to live for up to forty years again, living off their investments and savings. Therefore it's important to get started as early as possible because you are going to need to have saved a lot. As I tell my clients, pick a number that's at the edge of your comfort zone – it's a good thing if the commitment makes you tighten your belt!

If you die before seventy-five, your pension can go to whoever you want it to, tax free. If you die after seventy-five, the money can go to whoever you want it to, but they will have to pay tax as if it was theirs – don't worry though, they don't have to wait until fifty-five to touch it if they are younger.

Types of Pensions

State pension

The government provides a state pension for everyone, and the current age for claiming the state pension is sixty-seven, although this is set to increase. Unless you are a woman born before 1953 or a man before 1951, then you are eligible for the New State Pension.

To get a state pension you will need to have at least ten qualifying years of National Insurance (NI) contributions. You qualify for a year if:

- You paid NI because you were working

- You get NI credits, e.g. if you were ill, a parent (rules apply) or a carer

- You paid voluntary NI contributions

Currently the maximum New State Pension is £164.35 per week (as of June 2018), it is paid every four weeks and you need to have paid thirty-five years of NI contributions to qualify.

Could you live off just a state pension? The Department for Work and Pensions reported in 2017 that more than one million retirees are currently being forced to do just that. Take a look through your budget planner – what would you manage to pay for and what would have to go?

So, first things first, will you get to thirty-five years of NI contributions? If you are unsure what you have already you can order a statement called a BR19. A BR19 will tell you what you have already qualified for and what you are likely to get from the state in retirement.

Workplace pensions

When it comes to workplace pensions, there are broadly two types: Defined Benefit and Defined Contribution.

Defined Benefit

This is a type of pension where what you get out at the end is guaranteed and the employer (with some contribution from the employee) guarantees to meet the cost to make sure the amount is paid. These pensions are becoming scarce and are now mainly reserved for civil servants and public sector workers, e.g. teachers, NHS workers and the fire service. These pensions provide a guaranteed income for life that is linked to inflation regardless of how long you live. Amazing if you can get it!

How the income is worked out varies but here is a common example known as a sixtieth scheme – so for every year that you work you get 1/60th of your final salary. To keep the maths simple, let's say you do your full career in the same job and work for forty years. When you retire you are earning £60,000. Therefore you have qualified for 40/60th of your final salary of £60,000. So at retirement, you will have a guaranteed income for life of £40,000 per annum. To put this into perspective, to provide this kind of income out of an investment pot, you would need around twenty-five times that amount – £1,000,000!

I once met a teacher who was not in the teachers' pension scheme because he didn't think it represented good value. My advice to him was 'Join ASAP!'

Defined Contribution

These have replaced Defined Benefit schemes in most workplaces and with these pensions you know what you put in, but not what you get out. What you get out depends on the performance of the investments that you pay into. Given that so much is at stake, it is scary that almost everyone pays no attention to where their money goes and opts for the default fund. Your work pension scheme will give you a choice of investments to pick from. Some will give you a huge list and others will be very limited. Regardless of your offering, it is important to find out what you are in, what you can be in and the costs involved.

To get hold of this information, get your latest pension statement. You will usually find a direct telephone number for the team that deals with your scheme either at the top right-hand side of the first page, or at the very bottom of the last page. Also on the first page will be your client reference number/policy number. When you get through to the team that deals with your pension, here are some of the questions that you need to ask:

1) Which fund(s) am I in? Are you able to send me a fact sheet (for each one) so I can see where it is invested and how it has performed?

2) What other investments can I choose from, is there a cost to switch funds and how many times am I allowed to change funds?

3) Do you have any information that explains the risk of each of the funds?

Usually with a work pension, if you pay in, your employer will pay in. You really need to try to make sure you do what needs to be done to get the maximum contribution from your employer, i.e. if they will match contributions up to 5% then you should pay in 5% to get their 5%. If not, you are missing out on free money!

If you have collected several pensions over your career to date, you may want to consider consolidating them into one pot. Pension providers will not usually let you consolidate pension pots without advice, so you might wish to seek out a well-qualified independent adviser to help you with this (see the Resources section on p. 250). Consolidation usually comes with costs involved so you need to make sure you understand all the cons as well as the pros to moving.

Finally, if you have got lots of pots scattered around, it is important that you keep track of all of them. Keep the details of each scheme on your financial summary spreadsheet and each time you move house, make sure you inform the providers.

Personal pensions

If you are self-employed or just simply want to save extra (yes, this is allowed!) then you can opt for a personal pension. There are many different types, but here are a few of the most common:

- **Stakeholder:** These are pensions for which the government has capped the fees that are allowed to be charged. In the first ten years, the maximum charge is 1.5% and then it drops to 1%. These pensions tend to offer a limited fund choice and in today's market don't tend to be that competitively priced for what you get.

- **Personal Pensions:** These are usually the next step up quality wise. They tend to offer a wider fund choice, but it may still be limited to in-house funds and a few extra external provider funds. This does vary hugely though between providers.

- **Wrap Pensions:** A wrap account usually allows you to have a pension along with other investments, e.g. ISA and General Investment Accounts all in one place. They tend to offer thousands of funds to pick from and you pay a fee for the wrap, plus a separate fee for the investment, which varies depending on what you pick. I use these a lot when looking after my clients' money.

- **SIPPs:** Traditional versions of these are ideal for people who want to do the weird and wonderful in their pension (as long as it is within pension rules). For example, an owner of a company wants to buy a premises for their business within their pension. Yes, this is possible! You can't buy residential property but you can borrow from your pension like a mortgage. However, you can only borrow 50% of the value, i.e. if you have £500,000 in your pension, you can borrow

£250,000. With this approach you have to be careful not to have all your eggs in one basket.

Pensions and Non-earners

If you or your partner are not earning, this doesn't mean you can't have a pension. You can still pay in £240 per month and claim tax relief. The benefit of doing this rather than having all the pension planning in one person's name is that you can use both of your personal allowances and lower rate tax thresholds – thus reducing the total tax that you pay as a couple.

It would mean that the earner is saving into the non-earner's pension on their behalf. I know you are probably thinking this, so I will answer the question: if you are married and then get divorced, the pension will be taken into account and shared or offset against other assets. If you aren't married, this wouldn't necessarily be the case.

Part-time/Contract/Self-employed

Along with people who take prolonged periods of time out of work (e.g. to look after kids), those who work part-time, on a contract basis or are self-employed tend to be the ones whose pension planning is falling behind their full-time employed peers.

Let's break it down one by one.

Part-time

As you are working part-time your salary is going to be proportionally lower and so therefore is your pension planning if you and your employer pay in on a percentage basis. You need to work out how this will pan out in retirement – have a look at the projections your pension providers are sending you. Remember that they often assume you will keep paying in at the same rate all the way until retirement.

Contract

This could mean that you are in and out of pensions regularly with gaps in between. As you are not a full-time employee, you may also find that the amount your employer is paying in is the minimum contribution rather than the amount you should be paying in.

Some contractors (especially short-term contractors) are paid on a self-employed basis. So you might feel dizzy when you see the day rate but don't forget that this higher day rate is being paid so that you can compensate yourself for the lack of pension and other benefits you are not receiving.

Conversely, if your day rate doesn't pay you enough to provide yourself with the benefits you would have if you were employed, perhaps it's time to renegotiate. You can get online quotes to demonstrate the cost of income protection and life cover and, as you have read above, you should know what percentage of your income should be going into a pension.

How to Benefit from Compounding

'Compound interest is the eighth wonder of the world. He who understands it, earns it . . . he who doesn't . . . pays it'
   Albert Einstein

So this is where I introduce you to your secret weapon to retirement success – COMPOUNDING! This is where you have growth on growth and, to have really benefited, you need to get growth on growth on growth! To achieve this, your money needs as much time as possible to grow. Therefore you need to start paying in as soon as possible – and as much as possible.

If you pay in £100 per month gross between the ages of twenty and forty and then nothing afterwards, what do you think you will have at sixty?

The answer is £73,400.

Now what would happen if you saved £200 between the ages of forty and sixty? What do you think you would have at the end?

The answer is £70,800.

So even though you have physically saved twice as much in the second scenario, because the money hasn't had time to have the compounding magic work on it, you end up with less.

Self-employed

Recent research reported in *Professional Adviser* suggests that 45% of self-employed people do not have a pension. I would also say that in my day job at a wealth management firm even really successful entrepreneurs have remained ostriches when it comes to pension planning. When I explain to them the tax advantages, they kick themselves. Don't forget that you can take the decision out of it by setting up a direct debit from your business account so that the money is out of sight and tucked away in your pension fund.

Alternatives to Pensions

Pensions aren't the only way to save for your retirement. In fact, I actively encourage clients to build their wealth in various different tax wrappers, e.g. pensions, ISAs, General Investment Accounts, etc., to complement their pension planning. That way you can stay the right side of a tax threshold by taking pension up to the limit and then, if you need extra, taking it tax free from, say, an ISA.

The benefit of having something in everything is that over time the government will change its tax treatment of different investments, so when this happens you can switch to the most preferential option at the time.

Yes, that's right, you do pay tax in retirement. See the income tax diagram (p. 15) for a refresher. Your state pension, work and personal pensions, and rental income

Will Your Home be Your Pension?

A lot of people say that their house is their pension without really thinking about it. Is it really? Where would you live? Your house can only be your pension if you sell it and buy somewhere cheaper and live off the equity. Have a think – at current prices, what could you downsize to in an area that you would like to live in and how much money would this free up? How long would that money last?

The other way for your home to become your pension is if you do an equity release. Equity release is like the opposite of a mortgage. You have to be over fifty-five and you can release some of the cash tied up in your home. There are two types: Lifetime Mortgages and Home Reversion. With Lifetime Mortgages you can opt to pay back the money monthly or you can roll it up and pay it back on your death. This means that the debt can rack up quite quickly – especially if you live for a long time. Home Reversion is where you sell some of the equity in your home for a lump sum or regular income and you can stay in the property until you die. The downside is that you will typically get only 20–60% of the value of the part that you sell.

are all taxed in retirement above your personal allowance (the tax-free bit).

If you continue to earn whilst drawing your pension, pay extra attention to your tax to ensure that your pension doesn't go back to the taxman unnecessarily!

Getting Your Retirement Planning on Track

Now you have learned the basics, it's time to put this knowledge into action:

1) Do you have pensions scattered around? If so, make sure the providers have your correct address and ask them to send you a recent valuation, fund breakdown, details of the charges on the plan and a list of all the investments that you can invest in.

2) Be patient – some pension providers are really slow and as a way to protect you from pension fraud (i.e. someone stealing your pension) they may ask you to jump through hoops. If they do, it is worth it. It will only be harder to trace and to get things straight some years down the line when you come to retire.

3) Add the pension to your financial summary spreadsheet so you can keep track of everything.

4) Work out what you need. Imagine what you will be paying for in retirement and complete

a new retirement budget planner. Don't worry about getting this spot on. It is better to have a rough draft rather than nothing at all. Then over the years you can adapt it as your retirement expectations change.

5) If you have a work scheme, ask for a copy of the handbook. What do you have to pay in to get the maximum from your employer? Are you doing this? If not, why not? Push yourself to achieve this.

6) Now use a retirement calculator to see what you are projected to get. If you have Defined Benefit schemes, these calculators won't help with these. Keep them separate and add the total you expect to get at retirement to the figure when the calculator asks if you have any other income in retirement. You can get this figure from your most recent annual pension statement. Don't get carried away though – make sure you are looking at what you have accrued to date if you don't intend on staying with your employer until retirement.

7) Consider what you need to do to achieve your goal. How can you gradually work towards this? It is also *very* important to ensure that if you move jobs you get at least as good a pension – and, if not, that you get more

money in your salary so you can pay in more yourself.

8) Next, make sure the investment funds you are in are performing as you would hope. Find out the name of each fund and google the name along with 'trustnet' at the end. This should then show you where your fund is invested, across which region, and if it is outperforming its benchmark. If it is outperforming, great, but even if it's not it doesn't necessarily mean you should sell straight away. You need to understand why your investment is different. You may want to approach a financial adviser to help you pick which funds to sell and which to keep. An adviser will be able to help you work out which funds suit your attitude to risk.

If you would like to assess your attitude to risk, you will usually find a risk-profiling tool on your pension provider's website.

9) Remember, when thinking about the risk you can take with an investment, it is usually grossly overstated when you imagine it compared to what you would feel when it actually happens. When markets fall and my clients call me in a panic, I know that the first thing I should check is their attitude to risk. Perhaps they are taking more risk than they are actually comfortable with? Perhaps they underestimated

how worried they would feel? It has all been rosy in the markets for almost a decade, but now that's changed, can they take the rough with the smooth?

10) REVIEW – it is great that you have done this and got everything together, but I recommend that you set a six-monthly review in your diary to check your progress and to make sure you are working towards your target.

Have You Lost £400,000,000?

According to the government, there is £400,000,000 sitting in pensions that are unclaimed! Fortunately, the government has a pension tracing service to help – see the Resources section on p. 250 for their website. (When going online to check, do make sure you are on www.gov.uk, and not some other website.)

Can you believe there is so much money out there in pensions that goes unclaimed? This is only going to get worse, too, as a 'job for life' becomes a thing of the past. According to Baroness Ros Altman, the average person will have eleven jobs during their lifetime. That is a lot of pensions to keep track of!

The government has a really easy solution for you to trace your pensions and claim your share of this pot. Here's how:

1) Write up a list of all the employers you have worked for and approximate dates – this doesn't need to be exact.

2) Call up the Pension Tracing Service on 0191 215 4491 or visit their website.

3) Get in touch with the pension company using the details you have been given and send them your new contact details so they can stay in touch.

4) Review your long-lost pension: has it performed well, what are the costs, when will it pay out, what are the T&Cs?

A word of warning – there are a lot of companies out there that will charge you to find your pension. Why pay someone to do it for you when it really is as easy as the steps above?

Pension Jargon Buster

Annual Allowance: The maximum you can pay into a pension in any given tax year. The amount is set by the government. If your earnings are below the annual allowance, then you can only claim tax relief on pension contributions up to 100% of earnings.

Annuity: A fixed sum of money paid to you from your pension, typically each year for (usually) the rest of your life.

Defined Benefit Pension: Pays a retirement income based on your salary and how long you have worked at your company. Also known as a Final Salary Pension.

Defined Contribution Pension: You and usually your employer pay into a pension that is invested in funds. What you get back in retirement depends on how those investments have performed.

Flexi-access Drawdown: Allows you to use your pension to provide yourself with an income by taking out slices each year.

Lifetime Allowance: The maximum you can build up in a pension pot without paying a tax penalty.

Money Purchase Annual Allowance: The maximum you can pay into a pension each year once you have started to take an income out of your pot.

State Pension: The regular payment you receive from the government in retirement. The amount you get depends on your National Insurance record. You can start to claim your state pension when you reach state pension age, currently sixty-seven.

Tax-free Lump Sum: Sometimes referred to as a PCLS (Pension Commencement Lump Sum). This is the lump sum that you are allowed to take out of your pension tax free. Currently the rules allow you to take out 25%.

6

PLANNING FOR THE UNEXPECTED

Even the most meticulous of budgeters can be hit by unexpected costs and life's little blips that put their finances at risk of coming unstuck. The key here is to have well-thought-out contingencies for any worst-case scenarios that could put your budget in jeopardy, with a plan of action to get you back on track.

My Budget Just Got Derailed – Now What?

The most important thing here is not to let it derail you further. Rather than thinking, 'F*ck it! I might as well just go on a spending spree,' it is now time to tighten your belt and get back on track. Remind yourself of why you are being sensible in the first place – take a look at the goals you set at the beginning of the book.

It is also important to take some time to reflect, to see if the reason your spending was derailed was actually avoidable.

If you have hit a temporary speed bump with your budgeting – say you have had a blowout week – there doesn't need to be any long-term damage if you act quickly. Basic cost-saving principles need to kick in to make sure you get back on the road to good financial wellbeing:

1) Go back to basics – take your lunches into work, eat breakfast at home and have nights in. A little bit of old-fashioned money-saving will ensure the fallout from your blowout was only temporary.

2) Have a chat with your budgeting buddy (see p. 77) to help motivate you to stay on track and not stray further.

3) Look back at your money vision board for motivation, to remind yourself of the bigger picture and what you are aiming at.

If your budgeting detour hasn't been a blip, but you have in fact gone completely off the rails for a while, the first thing to do is reassess where you are. It is a great time to redo your budget and to make adjustments so that it is tricky to drop the ball again. Do you need to automate your finances better? Whatever the cause for going off track, it is time to get back to the basics discussed at the beginning of this book in the budgeting chapter. It is important to remind yourself of the goals you have set and what it will feel like when you have achieved your goals.

This is also a perfect time to organize yourself to be better in the future. A few little organizational tips can go a long way to making sure you are on the straight and narrow and not paying too much for things. Here are my top five tips:

1) Put the following dates in your diary:

- A reminder three months before your mortgage deal ends. This will prompt you to get in touch with an independent mortgage broker to ensure you get the best rate. If you rent, get in touch with your letting agent three months before your contract ends. What will be the costs involved in renewing the lease and will there be a rent increase?

- If you own a company, make a note of your company year end. Give yourself a warning six weeks before so you can consider extra pension payments to help reduce your tax and boost your retirement savings. If you are employed or a sole trader, the same applies at the end of the tax year.

- Do your personal tax return in May – set a reminder to prompt you. This is when your statements should start coming through from banks, pensions and investments. Set these aside in a special place as they arrive so you are not hunting them down. Doing it early will help you plan what you have to pay but will also mean that if you are due a rebate you will get it as early as possible.

- Have an 'October Organization' day. I set aside a morning each year to check my buildings and contents insurance, gas and electricity deals, and personal insurance, to make sure I have the right amounts and also that I am paying as little as possible.

2) Do a budget for the year each December. This is hugely important to work out what you can afford to spend big on, like buying a new laptop or going on holiday. It should also motivate you to work out what you can and should be saving and investing each month.

3) Increase your savings and retirement planning each time you get a pay rise.

4) In April each year, set aside an hour or two to review your savings/investments. Are you getting the best rate?

5) Make it easy to organize your paperwork. I am addicted to stationery and filing accessories so this comes a little too easily to me! But if this is an area you struggle with, investing in aesthetically pleasing stationery could be the key to your effective filing system.

What is my Back-up Plan If I Can't Work Because I'm Sick?

We would all like to think we are invincible and if we were too sick to work it might be nothing more than a measly bout of flu, but what if the unthinkable did happen? If you were unable to work, how would this affect your income and your budget?

Apparently 16 million people live with less than £100 in savings and 37% of households are a pay packet away from being unable to pay their rent or mortgage. Now these are scary figures, and really highlight the need for you to have a safety net if the worst were to happen. Those who are lucky enough to count themselves as 'rich' can self-insure – i.e. they have enough money to last for ever so whether they work or not is irrelevant. However, most people will need to use insurance to protect them if things go wrong.

Income Protection Insurance

We live in a world where the pet has great insurance, the dishwasher and washing machine have their own policies, but we often forget to insure our own income. If you are not automatically insured with work via an Income Protection policy, you really need to consider taking out a personal one.

Like all types of insurance, there are good and bad, and you only find out the real worth of the policy you have taken out when it comes to filing a claim. I would strongly recommend that you seek advice from an expert to help you find the right plan. Things to look out for are:

- It should pay out for as long as you need it to.

- There should be very few exclusions.

- The policy should be linked to inflation so that the value of your payout is not eroded over time.

- It should cover you if you can't do your particular job, rather than not being able to do any job.

The price of a policy will mainly be determined by your age, health, whether you smoke or not, how much cover you want and how long you want it for. To cover you for a few thousand pounds per month whilst you are young could cost you £30–£50. This would provide you a guaranteed income until you retire – for me, this is the most important financial planning product, and the first one I check to make sure that my clients have.

Critical Illness Cover

It is always a good idea to have some critical illness cover too if you can afford the premiums. Critical illness is different to income protection in that it will pay out a one-off lump sum on the diagnosis of a critical illness, e.g. cancer, heart attack or stroke. Most providers will cover you for tens of illnesses but it is best to shop around to make sure you are getting a really good-quality contract. I usually like it to cover a client's mortgage at least.

Life Cover

You only really need life cover if you have other people who are financially dependent on you – so if you have kids or a partner or spouse who couldn't afford to stay in their home if the mortgage wasn't cleared or they didn't have a lump sum to support them to pay the rent.

I always recommend that clients who need life cover first of all cover all their debts (including mortgage). If they are actively paying off their debts, e.g. a repayment mortgage, then they need to have cover on a decreasing basis. This means that over time as they pay off their debt, then the amount of cover they have is also decreasing. This is a great way to save money, compared with

Mobile			D.o.B			
Home			Smoker			
Email			Dependants			

Owner	Provider	Policy Number	Policy Type	Start Date	Maturity Date	Premium
					Totals	

Insurance

Savings

Pensions

Investments

Assets & Liabilities

	Value	Balance	Lender	Cost p.m.	Rent p.m.	Rate
Main Residence						
Secondary Residence						
Loan						
Will						

General Insurance

	Buildings	Contents	Motor 1	Motor 2	Travel	Pet
Provider						
Premium						
Expiry Date						

Occupation		Gross	
Company		Net	
NI		Date	

Status	Life Cover	Critical Illness Prepay.	Critical Illness	Redundancy	Income Protection	Value	Notes

Expiry Date	Minimum Rental Income	Equity	Notes

Prof. Indem.	Pub. Liability	Notes

having a level cover that would remain the same throughout the policy's existence.

On top of this you need life cover to meet family expenditure and the costs associated with maintaining the family standard of living. To work out what you need, look at your budget planner and see what your annual outgoings are without your mortgage (this is already covered by the decreasing policy mentioned above). You then need to multiply this annual figure by twenty to calculate a big lump sum – and yes, this really is what you need!

Before you apply for this amount of cover, you need to check if you have any cover at work and if so you may want to deduct this from your total need.

Finally, make sure your policy is linked to inflation so that the amount it pays out goes up each year and in turn so will the premiums.

When it comes to choosing a provider, you can choose the cheapest provider as long as the company is reputable and has a good credit rating. It is not as important to shop for quality as it is with income protection and critical illness cover because, well, once you're dead you're dead!

This is not very well known, but you should consider writing your life policy into trust. This is not anything fancy, it is just an extra form in the insurance application process and it means that if you die the money will pay out into a trust rather than into your own estate. The benefit of this is that it won't qualify for inheritance tax, but just as important, it is likely to pay out much faster at a time when your family don't need extra stress. For existing life policies, just call up your provider and ask them to send you the trust form for the policy.

If you already have existing insurances, it is important to work out what you have. Add the policy details to your financial summary spreadsheet and if you are not sure of the details, give your insurer a call to check you don't have the wrong end of the stick. For completeness, I also like to add my client's work benefits to this spreadsheet too so that everything is in one place for their partner/family.

Splashing Out: Planning Ahead for Expensive Moments

Impulse splashing-out moments should be the exact opposite! They should be well thought through, pre-saved for occasions that you know you can afford. This will help you to not only enjoy the big occasion, but also to not feel guilty about spending the money.

Christmas is very predictable – it happens every year and should be saved for throughout the year so you avoid the common debt hangover of January that a lot of people face. Usually weddings and other big events are also known about in advance and so money should be allocated from your budget each month to work towards saving for these expenses. Getting out of the negative

Occasion	When	How Much	Cost per Month

cycle of not being prepared and then feeling guilty about overspending is easily reversed by good planning.

If you are in the phase of your life when weddings and hen parties are a regular occurrence, I would pre-empt any invitations by committing to putting some money aside every month, way before the save-the-dates arrive.

So let's plan the big financial occasions you will have over the next twenty-four months.

If you don't end up spending all the money for each occasion, you can always roll it over into your next short-term goal/building up your emergency cash buffer/saving for a house deposit account.

7

MONEY AND RELATIONSHIPS: THE GOOD, THE BAD AND THE UGLY

As the saying goes, 'to be forewarned is to be forearmed'.

When my husband and I were in our twenties and not yet married, but were starting to get 'financially serious' together, we had an agreement drawn up with the solicitor when we bought our house that clearly stated what would happen if we were to split up. Fortunately, we didn't have to call on this agreement but it could well have been the best few hundred quid we had ever spent if we had split up. So how can you forearm yourself and your relationships?

How to Talk to a Partner About Money

As we noted earlier, money can be a taboo subject and people's relationship with it is often so heavily influenced by their upbringing that their views can sometimes be illogical and very difficult to unravel. This can create a lot of potential for arguments within a partnership. Here are my four top tips for how to talk to your significant other about your finances:

1) Talk about the good and the bad – start by talking through your financial dreams and what you would like to work towards as a couple.

2) Treat it like a business meeting and take turns to talk if it gets heated.

3) Make sure you both agree – it is very easy for the more vocal/more financially knowledgeable partner to dominate the conversation.

4) Just because you have discussed it once it doesn't mean the discussion is closed for ever. We all change over time so it is important to continue to keep the money dialogue open.

Use the space on the opposite page to plan what it is you want to ask or suggest to your partner. Writing it down will help to reduce the chances of an argument or not getting your point across accurately.

How Will Your Money Work Together?

It is really important to get a plan together that you are both happy with from the beginning. Don't forget that by combining your finances, you are both responsible for the good and the bad (i.e. debt). Here are some

questions you need to ask yourselves to help build financial trust between the two of you:

- Will you go the whole hog and have all money going into one account?

- Will you have a joint account that you each pay into and then have separate personal accounts for personal expenditure?

- Will you pay in different amounts towards the bills if you are earning very different amounts?

- What will happen to you as a couple if one of you isn't able to earn due to illness/injury? (Look back at the Income Protection section on p. 188 for a solution.)

- Who will manage the day-to-day spending? Ideally, you should be doing this together rather than relying on one person.

Being Honest About Your Debts

It is vitally important to be open and honest with each other. If you have any financial skeletons in the cupboard, it's time to fess up! Research by the Money Advice Service showed that nearly 30% of UK adults have been with a partner who has later divulged or let slip that they are in 'serious debt'. Worryingly, 18% also admitted they had actively hidden their debts from a partner.

There are other financial secrets too that you might

'Pink' Jobs and 'Blue' Jobs

In a quite embarrassing interview on the BBC, Theresa May and her husband talked about 'pink' jobs and 'blue' jobs. I know she was trying to appear more approachable and give us an insight into the real Theresa May, but I couldn't help but cringe at the time.

However, from what I see in my day job it does seem that more often than not money management falls into the 'blue' job category.

This has a huge impact in the event of the death or serious illness of a partner, a divorce or a break-up.

Even if money is not particularly interesting to you, it is important that you keep an interest in the finances if you are in a relationship and that you don't automatically delegate to your partner – even if they are naturally better at it. I think it is always good to point out that just because one person is better at it, it very often doesn't mean they are good at it. I have so many clients who can run huge companies but not their own finances!

wish to consider sharing with your partner. For example, quite a few of my clients don't tell their partner the extent of their assets, and I always feel uncomfortable about it, especially when their partner is in the room.

What if you find out your partner has debt?

This can be really tricky. You may feel at first that your partner has been deceitful by not telling you about their debt. No matter how cross you are, don't forget to consider their feelings too. They may be feeling hopeless and/or guilty, neither of which will be helpful in trying to sort the problem out.

If you feel that your partner has a serious debt problem, there are many debt charities out there that are willing to help, as we discussed in chapter 2 (see also the Resources section on p. 249).

Whether it's serious or not, it's important to help your partner formulate a plan to get out of debt and to not return to debt (especially without telling you). What was the reason for the debt? Perhaps as a couple you were spending too much and therefore you are partly culpable? Can you adjust your budgets accordingly to get back on track?

What To Do If You or Your Partner Earns Significantly More than the Other

Research by LV found that a quarter of women now out-earn their partners and that this imbalance can often lead to arguments. Reports additionally show that having less money than your partner and having to rely occasionally on them for financial support can make you feel a loss of control, guilty for being a burden or even lead to low self-esteem – all of which may start to chip away at the relationship.

As with most problems, it is important to talk about it. Find out what you both feel about the imbalance and decide together on what is and what isn't acceptable. Even if the finances are unequal, it's important that you find the equality in other ways in order to maintain a healthy relationship.

Here are some ideas on how you may choose to split your money:

- **Equal:** It will only be possible to split things equally if the imbalance isn't huge or as a percentage of your income you aren't spending very much.

- **In Proportion to Income:** If you agree together that the higher earner is happy to pay a higher percentage, you can split it proportionally. For example, if Partner 1 earns £35,000 and Partner 2 earns £30,000 then you could split the £2,500 per month bills as follows:

$$\text{Partner 1 pays } \frac{£2,500}{(£35,000 + £30,000)} \times £35,000 = £1,346.15$$

Partner 2 pays £2,500 − £1,346.15 = £1,153.85

What If One of You Decides to Make a Change That will Result in a Significant Salary Cut?

Again, this decision needs a joint conversation. How will this decision impact you both financially and what sacrifices will have to be made, both as individuals but also as a couple? To avoid any heated argument in the early days of this discussion, base your conversation on facts. Play around with your budget planner and imagine what your new life (no matter how temporary it is) will cost and what sacrifices will need to be made to make the books balance.

How important is this life change and are you/your partner likely to see it through? If this change is going to have a temporary financial impact, you both need to be sure it is the right thing to do and that it will take you in the direction you want your future to be heading. If the other partner is not on board or isn't willing to accept the sacrifices that would have to be made (perhaps they aren't happy with going back to the beans-on-toast student life), only the partner making the change can decide if they are being held back and if they are willing to take their new chosen path alone.

When Relationships Break Down

We need to be able to think clearly about the motives for a relationship breakdown and to make a decision with a clear head. I have met so many clients over the years who are staying in a relationship they are not happy with because money is keeping them there. For me this is really sad and a key driver to be financially savvy so that I can be relationship savvy.

The 'No Nup' Agreement

You have more than likely heard of a prenup – the legal agreement of choice for celebs and the well-heeled to protect their assets as much as possible before they marry in the event they divorce in the future. You might even have heard of a postnup, but a 'no nup' is an agreement that is drawn up between two individuals who aren't married to set out what would happen financially if they split up. Here's what you need to know:

- It is a 'living together' agreement for couples who aren't married or have no intention of marrying.

- It is essentially a contract between two people and so can be as detailed or as simple as you need it to be.

- It is particularly helpful if one person owns a property and they are both going to contribute to it together.

- It sets out clearly what would happen financially if you split up.

- It can detail who is going to pay what –
  i.e. bills, etc.

- You can get one drawn up by a solicitor,
  but the same solicitor can't represent both
  people.

So why are they important and getting more and more
press? According to the Office for National Statistics, the
number of couples cohabiting in the UK has doubled
in the last twenty years – it's currently 6.5 million. That
is a lot of unprotected people! Many people mistakenly
think there is such a thing as a common-law spouse,
but this is not true and definitely will not offer any financial protection to anyone living together should they
split up.

Separating Out Entangled Finances

Separating out finances from a partner's when you split
is always going to be tricky, especially if you have been
together a long time and if you have differing views on
who should have what.

When talking about the financial side of a split, it is
important to be as unemotional as possible, so perhaps
first test out having the discussion with a friend or relative who can help you see the other side of the story.
This will also allow you to recognize your trigger points
for being drawn into an argument – and hopefully avoid
this trap when it's time for the real thing.

Realistically, the cost of separation is never going to be cheap. When it comes to moving out, you are going to need to take into account the cost of setting up home again, e.g. a deposit for rental or a deposit for buying, and the cost of paying for a house all by yourself – not just the monthly mortgage or rent but the bills, food, etc.

One of the areas where I do a lot of work is helping to rebuild people's wealth back up after a separation or divorce. Even though it's a difficult time, it is really useful if you can assess the long-term impact of the split on your finances as soon as possible. Have you given assets away? With higher outgoings, are you still able to save/invest each month? How will the separation affect your immediate budget as well as your long-term financial goals? Revisit your financial goals and budget planner and adjust accordingly.

Divorce

The cost of a divorce can be HUGE! Court fees are hundreds of pounds and legal fees are likely to be at least several thousand. I have worked with clients whose legal fees have even run into hundreds of thousands of pounds. One way to really rack up this cost is to spend a lot of time speaking to your solicitor about your feelings, as they usually charge by the hour. Leave the solicitor to deal with what they are good at and use your friends/family or a counsellor to help you work through the emotional side of the divorce.

Moving Out of a House Share

Entangled finances aren't just restricted to romantic partnerships though – plenty of housemates and friends also find themselves needing to cut their ties with each other at certain points in their lives. For example, when you move out of a house share you may not think this would impact your finances, but have you considered the costs involved not only with the physical move, but other areas where your outgoings will also be affected? These will have a knock-on effect on your budget. Most importantly, always read your tenancy agreement in FULL before you sign it. If you haven't, then you should do it now. There might be some nasties in there that could trip you up.

Before moving out you need to know whether you are sole or joint tenants. According to the Money Advice Service, if you are the sole tenant then anyone else living there is your guest. If you are joint tenants you are responsible for paying the rent until the tenancy agreement is altered.

You will need to order statements from your utility providers to work out what your share of the bills will be until the day you leave. Make sure your housemates agree with the way you have calculated it so that you don't fall out over the small stuff. If you haven't been using one already, there are some great apps out there to take the pain out of splitting the bills. This is the stuff dreams are made of – take a look at the app Acasa (formerly known as Splittable).

I have already mentioned that having joint accounts can have a negative impact on your credit rating. So if you are moving out and you have had joint finances, it is important to check (and double-check) that the account has been closed. To be extra careful, always write to the credit reference agencies and ask for a notice of disassociation to ensure that you are no longer connected financially.

You will also need to make sure you are financially prepared to move into your new property:

- Make sure your contents are covered from the day you move in. You don't want them being stolen as you transport them from the van to the flat – especially if you are not covered!

- Check your deposit is protected by a deposit protection scheme – this is now a legal requirement for landlords (and agents).

- You may be moving to a new place that you know you can afford, but have you looked into the cost of travel? If you are in a new area this could be very different to what you were paying before.

- Make sure you are 100% aware of what bills you must pay, e.g. is council tax included or are you obliged to pay this?

- It is always a good idea to save up whilst you are living in the property to have money set aside for your moving costs, e.g. hiring a man and a van.

- If your contract includes 'joint and several liability' then the landlord has the right to chase the remaining tenants for the shortfall in rent if someone does not pay their share.

Before you vacate your property it is important to know what your check-out obligations are, for example, you may need to have the carpets professionally cleaned, so check your tenancy agreement. This will ensure that you have the best chance of getting your full deposit back. You will probably want to take photos when you leave as proof that you left it in a good state to avoid any disputes. Your landlord must give your deposit back within ten days of getting it back from the tenancy deposit scheme.

8
PASSING IT ON

Talking about death really is a taboo subject, one we often shy away from at all costs, but death and your money is something very important to think about. You need to put together a 'When I'm Dead' file whilst you are still alive. This is usually something that most people put off until 'they are older' and then it becomes one of those jobs that doesn't happen. Here are the things you will need to put in it:

1) A summary of your life insurances – which provider they are with and how much they would pay out. Make it easy and add the contact details to the front. If you have written the policies in trust, have a copy of the trust in the file too.

2) Details of any life cover that you have at work – add the amount and the contact details of the HR person/phone number at work who would help with the payout.

3) A summary of all assets and debts including pensions, investments, etc. – insert a copy of your financial summary spreadsheet.

4) A copy of your will and your solicitor's contact details.

5) The contact details of your financial adviser if you have one.

Something else to consider is that recently solicitors have started to talk a lot about your digital footprint on your death. According to UK Report in 2016, a typical internet user has more than a hundred separate online accounts – just think about how many social media sites, online banking and shopping accounts you have logins to. The study also identified that this number would double by 2020!

Now some of these will be classed as digital assets and will form part of your estate when you die, so it is vital that executors of your estate are able to gain access to these assets too. Examples of digital assets are online bank accounts and purchase sites, PayPal, Amazon, eBay, etc.

Solicitors that I have spoken to say that the UK law needs to catch up with our needs when it comes to digital assets as each website will have different rules that the executors will have to trawl through. To make their job a little easier, make sure that all digital assets are mentioned in your 'When I'm Dead' file.

Making a Will

If you die without a will, you die intestate. This means that intestacy laws determine what will happen to your money and assets when you die. This may or may not be what you want to happen. The only way to ensure your money goes to the people you want it to on your death is to write a will. The fundraising campaign Will Aid estimates that more than half of British adults don't have a will, but writing one is particularly important in today's world, especially when it comes to the blended family. Of course, there are lots of templates out there that you can use for very little money, and done properly these are better than not having one at all. But a will needs to be formally witnessed and signed to make it valid, and mistakes can be hugely costly if you get it wrong – both emotionally and financially. It's important to remember that a marriage will void a will. So if you make a will whilst single and then marry, this will cause the will to become void. You can add a clause about any anticipated marriage to ensure the will remains effective, but otherwise you will need to do a whole new one.

Inheritance Tax

The purpose of inheritance tax is supposed to be so the rich don't always remain rich and so that people's wealth is redistributed equally across society.

Inheritance tax is paid on death at 40% on assets above £325,000. If you are married you get to use each other's allowance, so that on the death of the second person you have an allowance of £650,000. If you give 10% of your estate to charity though you will only pay tax at 36%.

So if, for example, your parents are married and all their assets total £700,000, they will only pay inheritance tax on the £50,000 above the £650,000. There is one caveat to this rule: there now exists a 'main residence' band, which is valid on a main residence where the recipient of a home is a direct descendant (child, step-child or grandchild). The rules are being phased in until April 2020 and eventually will give each person an extra £75,000 (i.e. a total of £500,000 per person – £1million for a married couple). On properties between £1million and £2million you will pay tax at 40% on everything above £1million. On properties worth over £2million, the rules are different: you lose £1 of the main residence allowance for every £2 of the value above £2million.

Everyone pays inheritance tax unless your job qualifies as a 'risky role' and an injury that you suffered during active service has impacted your life expectancy. People

such as those in the armed forces, paramedics, firefight-
ers and the police fall into this category.

You have to pay inheritance tax by the end of the
sixth month after a person dies. So if someone dies in
January you have to have paid the tax by the end of July.

Where Does Debt Go When We Die?

Sadly, debts still have to be paid on death. There is an
order in which they have to be paid. Firstly, secured debts
(e.g. a mortgage or a loan against your car). Secondly,
funeral costs and admin costs for managing and distrib-
uting your estate. Next are unsecured debts (e.g. personal
loans). However, you can only inherit someone's debt if it
was a joint debt and you were already liable.

As We Age

As we age, life brings with it new financial obstacles to
navigate and whether you have accumulated sufficient
assets and how much you have will determine a lot of
what you do and don't have to pay for.

Paying for Health Care

In the UK, we are really fortunate that access to the NHS
is free. For all situations where I have used the service, they

have been amazing. However, I have also opted to have private medical insurance for me and my family as back-up. If you are considering whether or not to invest in such cover yourself, here are a few things to know:

- The price of medical insurance will usually change on renewal and most insurance policies are annual contracts. Typically they tend to increase by 3–5% each year.

- You will have access to more resources than the NHS can offer you and it means that you don't have to wait as long as you would on the NHS.

- You choose which hospital you go to and even which doctor you want to treat you.

- Location can have a huge impact on what you pay. For example, if you have central London hospitals available to you, this can really bump up the cost.

- If you switch to a new provider, you need to make sure they will cover your pre-existing conditions.

- Incurable and chronic conditions are not usually covered.

- If you have a policy through your work, it's important to remember that if it's company paid, you may well be liable to pay tax (P11D) on the benefit.

Paying for Social Care

Paying for social care might not feel like something that's relevant to you as an individual right now, but it's still worth knowing about now as it may be of concern to you when thinking about your parents and grandparents.

No social care is completely free. What you pay for depends on what you need and what assets you have to support yourself already.

Homecare support provides help with everyday tasks such as getting in and out of bed, washing and preparing meals. Most councils charge for these services, and they will have procedures in place to work out what you can and can't afford to pay.

Adaptations to your home can help to make things more manageable. Usually specialist disability equipment is provided for free, and if the council recommends minor adaptations, these can also be free if they cost less than £1,000, e.g. ramps, a dropped kerb or grab rails. If larger adaptations are needed, you can apply for a Disabled Facilities Grant to help with these costs.

Paying for Care Homes and Specialist Housing

Paying for a care home is very expensive – Age UK have calculated that the average cost is around £600 a week for a care home place, and over £800 a week for a nursing home. Getting financial help from the government can be very complicated and difficult to navigate too. If you need help paying for a care home you will be means tested and the government allows you to have a whopping £24.90 left per week. This is called the Personal Expenses Allowance. Your assets are also taken into account and if you have £23,250 (correct at 2018) or more, then you must pay your fees yourself. If you have less than £14,250, these savings are ignored and the local council will pay for your care, but they will still take your income into account. Between these two figures the council will fund some of the care. The value of your home is included in the means test (minus any loan/mortgage and 10% of its value to cover expenses if you were to sell). The home won't be counted though if your partner is living there, a relative over sixty is living there, a relative that is disabled or a child under eighteen resides there.

If in doubt, it is important to check if you (or your family members) are eligible for any benefits too. If you need help with care, you may find that you are eligible for a disability benefit, either Personal Independence Payment or Attendance Allowance. Neither of these are means tested so your savings and income won't be taken into account.

Paying for a Funeral

The average funeral apparently costs more than £4,000 and so it can be a worry for family members to find this money at an already difficult time. A lot of funerals are pre-paid by the deceased using a funeral plan which they took out when alive. Funeral plans differ so it's important to check what is and what is not covered. You could also take out an insurance policy that pays out on death, such as the over-fifty plans that you see advertised on daytime TV. There is also a government funeral payment of £700 that can be applied for by those with a low income.

9

ONCE IN A LIFETIME

So now you have done the hard work – set your goals, managed your budget and debts, thought about your retirement – let's talk through the fun stuff! As I said at the beginning of the book, your money should be the thing that gives you the life you want, not the thing that dictates your life. It might be helpful to reflect back on your goals and also your money mood vision when reading this chapter.

That Dream Holiday

I love it when a client's goal list is jam-packed full of exciting travel plans. After all, life is for living! I also believe that having big goals and dreams helps to motivate you to get serious about the small financial decisions, so that you can afford the dream trip you have always promised yourself.

Like any goal, the better you have prepared for it the more likely it is to happen, so you need to know:

- When are you going?

- Who is going with you?

- How much will it cost?

- How long are you going for?

- What impact will this have on other areas of your life, for example, what would happen with your job if you took months off?

Record your answers here:

A lovely friend of mine had a great job at a magazine but she was determined to go travelling for three months with her boyfriend. She was prepared to quit, but managed to negotiate with work that she would take an unpaid sabbatical along with some of her holiday entitlement and her job would be there when she got back. So it's important before asking for something like this to arm yourself with the facts. Has anyone done anything similar before? Is there a sabbatical policy after X years of service in your contract? If you don't think you could ever ask for such a thing, remember, if you are a valuable asset to your company you shouldn't underestimate the cost and hassle of replacing you!

If you are self-employed or a freelancer, there is perhaps more scope for you to take time out without it impacting on your business. Perhaps the trip could even make you money?

Once you've decided where and when you want to go, you need to add the dream holiday to your goals list and start saving. If the dream holiday is less than five years away, the only thing you can do is to start saving monthly in cash or perhaps Premium Bonds. If the holiday is more than ten years away then you may want to invest some of the money to try and get a better return. Adapt your budget planner to accommodate this goal and prioritize the monthly commitment over ad hoc purchases that you can do without.

Giving Up Work to Retrain or Changing Careers

Again, it is really important to use your money to make you happy and to choose the path in life that fulfils you. I couldn't imagine being a 'wage slave' and dreading going to work. Therefore, if you have to take time out to retrain or take a pay cut to start at the bottom of a new industry and work your way up, it might just have to be done. But financial preparation can help to make all that easier. Here are some questions you should work through to help you tally up the financial impact:

1) What will your new income be and what does the future look like paywise? Will you be eligible for a promotion and rise in six months' time? A year? Two years?

2) Play around with your budget planner. What changes would you need to make to ensure that you aren't relying on debt?

3) Will you have to live off savings? If so, for how long and what will you be left with? Is this acceptable to you?

4) Are there any big life changes you can make to help out financially? Move back in with your parents? Rent a smaller room/place or move to a cheaper area?

5) Are there any grants/funding that you can apply for? You might be eligible for educational grants and there are also bursaries available for teaching, social work and from the NHS.

Starting Your Own Business

Taking your money to the next level and how you do this really depends on what you want from life. What all my clients have in common who have earned their money (as opposed to inherited it or won it) is that they were willing to make those sacrifices needed in order to achieve financial success. They were willing to take the financial risk in the first place, whether this was taking out a loan against their home, going without a salary while the business was growing or downsizing their lifestyle temporarily to invest in their new venture. On top of this there are often big personal sacrifices too: the curse of the business owner is that you are never not working! Your switch is always on and leaving your work at your desk each evening just doesn't happen (especially in the early days). These clients are resilient and often stubborn when it comes to making their vision happen. I love helping entrepreneurs with their money because it often feels like their brains are wired differently – their thought processes start and end at very different places to most. I am often dumbfounded by their clarity around the direction they are travelling and, without doubt, they all know the answer to why they are doing what they are doing and what direction their life is heading.

So although most people would love the upside of running their own business, does this justify the downside? If you were to set up your own (or a new) business, what would you do? What would it look like? What could you be doing now on the side to get things going? Do you have any contacts that have useful experience who you could invite to lunch to pick their brains?

Use the space opposite to make some notes in answer to these questions.

Setting up your own business isn't something to just dive into. Bloomberg's statistics show that eight out of ten entrepreneurs who start their businesses fail within the first eighteen months. Added to this, Barclays recently discovered that female entrepreneurs are less successful at securing funding than their male counterparts: men are 86% more likely to get venture capital funding and 56% more likely to get angel investing. However, there is light at the end of the tunnel: Barclays also found that women entrepreneurs bring in 20% more revenue with 50% less money invested and that we are less likely to see our businesses go under, so women shouldn't be deterred! Perhaps we just need to give a little more fight along the way.

So would you like to do your own thing? Complete as many of the questions below as you can. It is really important to start thinking about it (if it's something you would

like to do) even if you don't have a firm and final idea for your business yet. Asking yourself these questions will put the business in the forefront of your mind, which will help you to spot potential opportunities.

What are the pros?

....

....

....

What are the cons?

....

....

....

Have you got an idea?

....

....

....

Could you do what you are doing now but on your own? Would you make more money/have more time?

....

....

....

What would setting up on your own give you that you don't already have?

....

....

....

What are the barriers to doing it?

....

....

....

Who do you know that can help you?

....

....

....

What training and education can you do/would you need to do? Can you start that now?

....

....

....

If you have decided to take the plunge and set up on your own, here is a step-by-step guide to how to get going:

1) Register yourself as a business. You can choose from one of these options:

   - **Sole Trader:** This is the simplest kind of organization but you are personally responsible for the business's debts if you get into trouble. You can register as self-employed via www.gov.uk.

   - **Limited Company:** You are not personally liable as your finances are separate from those of the business but you have a lot more reporting and management responsibilities, which usually leads to higher accountancy fees.

   - **Partnership:** A simple way for two or more people to run a business together. You share the responsibility of the debt together.

2) Get insured. You will need to protect yourself against risk, e.g. accidents, theft, being sued. I would recommend using an insurance broker so that you are sure you have got the cover you need.

3) Get a name. You will need this to be able to buy the website domain, print stationery, etc. Check Companies House to see if there are any other businesses that already have your name.

4) Get a bank account. Even if you are just starting off small as a sole trader, I would always recommend that you keep a separate bank account so that you are not spending money personally that you shouldn't be.

5) Play by the rules. Are you on top of data protection, the regulations for your industry and health and safety, for example? If your industry has a trade body, they will be able to help you to get compliant.

6) Get an accountant and start keeping track of everything that you spend – I keep a receipts wallet in my handbag so that they are all immediately kept together rather than having to hunt around at the end of the tax year.

7) Set targets. Whether you make or exceed these targets or not in the first year is not as important as knowing where you want to be heading and measuring yourself against it.

When You've Made Your Millions

Whether through a series of savvy financial decisions or that much-coveted lottery win, when it comes to advising people with *lots* of money, the framework isn't that much different to when I advise most 'regular' people. You still need to do the basics well before doing the complicated things in order to make sure your money works for you. Here are my top five tips to coping successfully with all that money:

1) Don't make too many changes too quickly.

2) Don't shout it from the rooftops.

3) Let the dust settle before you make any big financial decisions.

4) Surround yourself with the best independent advisers you can – shop around and get references. Pick someone you feel you can ask any question, however 'stupid' it might seem.

5) Don't forget that this is your money – just because you now have more of it, don't be pushed into making a decision that doesn't feel right.

Taking a Risk: Investing Your Money

A lot of people's minds go straight to investing when they think of financial planning. If you have followed the advice in this book so far, you'll know you need three pots of money: for the short term, medium term and long term. The short-term pot of money is your emergency cash buffer that we discussed in chapter 3 and the long-term pot of money is your retirement planning (usually a pension), which we covered in chapter 5.

Your medium-term pot could comprise of savings (covered in chapter 3) but also investments. When it comes to investing, it is important to remember that a little bit of knowledge can be a dangerous thing. If in doubt, seek advice from someone independent who you can understand and who you can see helping you in the long term (see the Resources section on p. 250 for links).

First Things First

- Make sure you have sorted out your short-term and long-term pots before you do your medium-term investment pot.

- Look at your budget planner and work out what is disposable.

- Is there anything you can cut back on to increase this budget?

- Do you feel confident you can put this money away and not touch it for at least five years?

Understanding Your Risk Tolerance

If you have got this far, you have decided that you can put some money away and you think doing so is a good thing for your financial future. But have you thought about how you would feel if things went wrong? It is well documented that most people feel more pain from a loss compared to the joy from an equal gain. Therefore it is important to get your investments right so that you can stick with it through the good *and* the bad. We all know that markets go up and down but staying disciplined in the bad times is often easier said than done. See the Resources section on p. 250 for help on how to assess your own attitude to risk.

Why Invest? The Difference Between Saving and Investing

People often get the two mixed up but it is important to be clear on the difference. When saving, you are aiming to get interest. Interest is a guaranteed amount that you know you will get from your bank or building society, like the ISAs we covered in chapter 3. Investing, on the other hand, is not guaranteed: what you get back depends on what you invest in and how long you invest it for. You could see a positive return or you may see a negative return.

When it comes to investment, people usually have higher expectations of the return they are aiming for. They want to be rewarded for the risks they are taking. Most investors are at least hoping for a net (after fees and tax) return higher than inflation.

When Not to Invest

You should never invest with short-term horizons in mind. So if what you are saving for is less than five years away, then your only option is to keep your money in cash. It would be sod's law that the moment you wanted to take the money out of your investment, the markets plummeted. This would cause you to either sell at a loss or to have to wait until markets have rebounded. By this time, you could have missed out on the perfect house, or the time to take that dream holiday has been and gone.

Having access to your cash can be important when it comes to your emergency cash buffer, but if you are investing for the medium/long term, access becomes less of an important criterion. Savings allow you this flexibility (unless you have tied it up), whereas due to the volatility of the market, you can't always be sure that you can access the money you have invested in at a profit or for at least what you have paid in.

How to spot a scam

If it seems too good to be true, it usually is! If you are being offered huge returns for a very safe investment, there has to be a catch. Why aren't the providers of the investment keeping all of those huge guaranteed returns for themselves?

Did they contact you? If you received a cold call, this should be a huge warning sign, along with unsolicited emails (usually with very poor grammar and spelling) and letters. If the investment is not regulated by the Financial Conduct Authority and it goes wrong, you won't have a leg to stand on.

If in doubt, don't do it!

Could You Fall in Love With Volatility?

Recently the financial markets have been hugely volatile and things are looking to stay this way. However, I haven't yet had one call from existing investors voicing any concerns. Hopefully they have comfort in the fact that their money is invested for the right reasons in the right things and that their investment risk perfectly matches their appetite for risk.

Of course, this is not always the case for self-investors or those with a pension pot that is not professionally managed. So how do you prepare your investments so that you can still enjoy a good night's sleep?

- Have you got the right investment for your risk? If it is a work pension that you have, spend some time on the website looking at your investment options. There should be a booklet that shows you which ones are suitable for you.

- Make sure you are taking the right level of risk. When you are young, you want to be taking the most amount of risk that you feel comfortable with when it comes to pension planning. This is because you have a long time until you can touch your pot – i.e. decades! If you are investing in, say, an ISA for a more medium-term goal, then you need to make sure you are taking the shorter term into account. A lot of my clients have different risk ratings for their ISAs and pensions, for example.

- Don't have all your eggs in one basket. If your investments are well diversified across the world and across different types of investments, then a dip in one market won't have such a huge impact on your pot. If you don't know where to begin with this you might want to start researching multi-asset funds.

Something to think about . . . If you are investing in the right things, for the right reasons, and the markets fall, are you brave enough to invest more?

Different Types of Investments

There are many different ways that you can invest, but let's start with the basics.

The most common way to invest is to pick funds. A fund is a collection of lots of investments that suit the fund's objectives, e.g. a UK Equity fund will be made up of hundreds if not thousands of UK stocks and shares.

A range of funds are then picked to create a portfolio. Most portfolios typically include the following asset classes (a category of investments that exhibit similar characteristics):

- **Equities:** These are stocks and shares. Equities are the higher risk element of the portfolio and help the portfolio to grow above inflation over the medium to long term, the downside being that when the markets are hit or there is a recession, equities are likely to fall.

- **Property:** Commercial property tends to be included in a portfolio as a smallish percentage. Commercial property includes office blocks, factories, medical centres, hotels, shopping centres, warehouses, etc. As it is not easy to sell a whole building when markets are falling, commercial property tends to be illiquid. In other words, you can't sell them easily. This is because in market downturns the fund temporarily closes to buying and selling to protect existing investors.

- **Government Bonds:** These are loans to a government. Government bonds are issued by countries to raise money and typically pay you a fixed return every six months (a coupon) for a certain period of time. A less economically stable country will need to pay a higher annual return than a country that is thought of as stable. Gilt is the name of a UK Government Bond. Traditionally, bonds are included in a portfolio to act in the opposite fashion to equities. They are typically thought of as the 'safe' part of a portfolio, although the current economic climate has turned this theory on its head.

- **Corporate Bonds:** These are the same as government bonds, but rather than lending your money to governments, you are lending the money to companies. The bond is only as good as the company you are lending to. Companies, like governments, issue the bonds as a way to raise money.

- **Cash:** Exactly what you would expect. Cash is held in a portfolio to pay fees for the investments and also if an investor is waiting for a buying opportunity. Keeping large amounts of cash in an investment portfolio for too long is dangerous because of the effects of inflation, the fact that the return offered is likely to be very low (or zero) and also because you may find you are paying fees to have the money in cash.

239

– **ISAs:** We talked about ISAs as a way of tax-free saving in chapter 3, but ISAs are also important when it comes to investing. If your investments grow in value and/or pay you dividends then if those investments are in an ISA they grow (almost) tax free.

There are lots of other asset classes that are sometimes included too:

– **Private Equity:** This is a bit like *Dragons' Den*. Private equity specialists invest in companies they believe can be turned around or vastly improved with an injection of cash. The end goal is to make big returns. A private equity fund will be made up of lots of companies. By their very nature, smaller companies are often high risk as they may go bust more easily than a large company that has been around for centuries.

– **Hedge Funds:** These typically have free rein to invest in whatever is deemed appropriate at the time. They often leverage their investments, i.e. rather than putting all of their own money into an investment they borrow money to put in. This has the effect of then amplifying actual returns or losses. They are typically used by sophisticated investors and/or the very wealthy.

– **Gold:** You may be investing in companies that produce gold or actual gold bullion. Investing in gold is used by investors as a hedge against inflation or geopolitical instability. As we saw, the gold price rallied after the credit crunch as investors fled to gold for a safe haven. The rush of investors to gold pushed up its price.

— **Index Linked Bonds:** These bonds pay out a return that is determined by inflation (usually CPI). They are used to protect an investment portfolio against inflation. They are usually offered by governments, e.g. the UK and US.

— **Commodities:** A raw product or agricultural produce that can be bought and sold. Examples include oil, grain, beef and natural gas.

Passive Versus Active

There are two (very) general rules of thumb when it comes to investing. Passive investing tracks the market up and down and as there is very little human intervention it is a very cheap way to invest. Advocates of this investment style feel that no one person/company can continually have good ideas over the medium to long term and therefore you are best to track the market, saving money along the way.

The other school of thought is active investing. This is where you believe in the value an individual or team can have on your investment and you are willing to pay a higher fee for this expertise. There are some superstar fund managers who would say that they prove their worth (but also some average ones who would say that too!).

Typically I tend to use passive investing at the start of someone's investing journey whilst the portfolio is small. This keeps the costs low.

Pound Cost Averaging

This is such an important investment principle that it is really worth getting your head around – so take as long as you need to fully get to grips with it.

Most people love the idea of being a trading demon and buying at the bottom of the market and selling at the top. The reality is very different and I have seen far too many portfolios where people have made massive errors and have lost a fortune. This is basically gambling rather than investing.

A much more considered approach is to commit to paying in monthly and sticking with it through thick and thin. What a lot of people initially struggle with is why you should continue to pay in if the market is falling and looks like it will continue to do so. The question you should be asking yourself at this moment is if what you are investing in is fundamentally a good investment. If so, you should keep with it. As we know, markets go up *and* down. If this statement is to continue to be true, you can reasonably expect the portfolio of investments that you are in to go back up sometime in the future (hopefully the not-too-distant future). If this is the case, the reason you continue to invest is that when you are buying in a falling market, you are effectively buying when the sale is on. You are buying investments cheaply.

How to Stay on Track

- Track performance regularly – but not too regularly! Try to look at your investment performance against the benchmark every six months. If you check it more than this (I do have clients who track several times a day!) you run the risk of getting too bogged down in the short-term fluctuations rather than the medium- to long-term goals that you have in mind.

- If you don't know where to begin, take a look at www.trustnet.com. This website will help you to look at your funds' performance compared to a benchmark. If your investment is underperforming compared to the benchmark, perhaps it's time to do a lot more research to understand why and to begin to look for alternatives.

- Transfer money into your ISA allowance every year. Making sure you are using your available ISA allowance each year ensures that any gains you make are all yours and that a proportion of the gains isn't given to the taxman.

- Rebalance your portfolio. If you initially set out to have say 50% of your money in equities and equities has a really good year compared to the other assets in the remaining 50% then, at the end of the year, you will have more than 50% of your money in equities. This could mean therefore that you will be taking more risk at the end of the year than perhaps you wanted to. Rebalancing means selling assets that you have too much of and buying the assets that you have too little of. You can usually preprogramme your investments to do this automatically should you wish to.

- Continue to assess your attitude to risk. It's important to check you are still doing the right things for the right reasons. As your time horizons change, it is important to see if you can still afford to take the same levels of risk. For example, if originally you were investing for a goal that was twenty years away (e.g. a holiday home at retirement) and now it is only two years away, you perhaps would now have a completely different attitude if your investment fell by 10% compared to how you would have felt eighteen years ago. I always assess a client's attitude to risk annually.

WHAT NOW?

Now we have come to the end of our money lessons together, I want you to review everything you have learned so far. My aim was to get you thinking about what was important to you rather than just meandering along without a clear life plan, and to arm you with the right tools to change your money habits for the better in order to reach these goals. If you look back at the beginning of the book, have your aspirations changed? Can you recognize areas where your thinking has now been transformed when it comes to your money?

Make a note here of some of your views that are now different when it comes to thinking about your financial wellbeing:

The most important takeaway message that I wanted to give you with this book is that good money management is a complete and long-lasting lifestyle change, rather than a fleeting fad diet. It is something you should be continually reviewing and building on as your life develops.

Write down three things you will now change straight away in order to work towards better financial wellbeing:

You should now have successfully created a budget planner, a financial summary of what you have and what you owe, and a list of the goals you are working towards. My biggest wish is that you are no longer sticking your head in the sand when it comes to dealing with your finances, that you feel more in control, open and positive when it comes to talking about money, and hopefully liberated from the stress of worrying about money; that your fear has been replaced with savvy financial know-how and you are keen to learn more.

I would recommend that you continue your learning by reading the Sunday money supplements every weekend, downloading money podcasts for your commute and working hard to find the right budgeting buddy for you so that you can support each other through the different financial stages of your life.

This book is something you can come back to time and again as new financial decisions crop up, to remind yourself of motivations, set new goals and help to plan and budget for any big financial changes. Remember, giving time and space to think and deal with your money is just as important an act of self-care as carving time out to relax, see your friends or hit the gym. It will give you the control you need in order to make your money work the best and get what you want out of life. Good luck on the next stage of your money journey!

RESOURCES

Useful Websites

Mortgages and buying a home

www.moneyadviceservice.org.uk/en/tools/house-buying/mortgage-affordability-calculator

www.bbc.co.uk/homes/property/mortgagecalculator.shtml

It may be helpful to check out further advice on the gov.uk websites on stamp duty: www.helptobuy.gov.uk

www.moneysavingexpert.com/mortgages/mortgage-overpayment-calculator

www.gov.wales/funding/fiscal-reform/welsh-taxes/land-transaction-tax/?lang=en

www.gov.scot/Topics/Government/Finance/scottishapproach/devolvedtaxes/LBTT

Debt

Christians Against Poverty offer a free debt-counselling course. See: www.capuk.org

The Samaritans: tel. 116 123

Citizens Advice: www.citizensadvice.org.uk

StepChange: www.stepchange.org

www.turn2us.org.uk

Unbiased financial advice

www.unbiased.co.uk
www.moneysavingexpert.com

Interest Rates

www.tradingeconomics.com/united-kingdom/interest-rate

Check Your Credit Rating

www.experian.co.uk
www.checkmyfile.com
www.equifax.co.uk

Pensions

www.gov.uk/government/publications/application-for-a-state-pension-statement
www.unbiased.co.uk
www.findpensioncontacts.service.gov.uk/declaration

Check Your Attitude To Risk

www.standardlife.co.uk/c1/guides-and-calculators/assess-your-attitude-to-risk.page

Investing

www.nutmeg.com/
www.moneyfarm.com/uk/
Moola: https://moo.la

Radio

BBC Radio 5 Live: *Wake Up To Money*
BBC Radio 4: *Money Box*

Podcasts

FT Money Show
She's On The Money (I am on this one so I had to include it.)
Meaningful Money – Pete Matthew
The Financial Wellbeing Podcast

Money to the Masses
The Property Podcast
Cash Chats – Andy Webb

Magazines

Money Week
Investors Chronicle

ACKNOWLEDGEMENTS

I would like to thank Aimee Longos for making this book a reality. It was just a throwaway comment and a thought on my commute this time last year. Thank you too to Toby for being patient with me whilst I was a ball of stress in the summer of 2018!

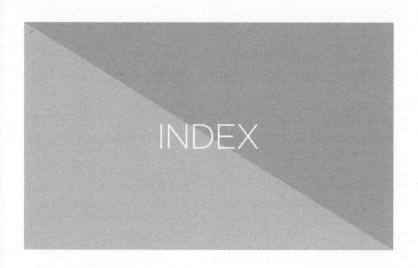

INDEX